Those PREACHING Women

VOLUME 4

DATE DUE

Those
PREACHING
Women

VOLUME 4

Edited by
Ella Pearson Mitchell and
Jacqueline B. Glass

JUDSON PRESS
Valley Forge

Those PREACHING Women, Volume 4

Unless otherwise noted, Scripture is taken from *The Holy Bible*, King James Version. (KJV). Other Bible quotations in this volume are from the following versions: HOLY BIBLE: *New International Version*, copyright © 1973, 1978, 1984. Used by permission of Zondervan Bible Publishers. (NIV); The New King James Version. Copyright © 1972, 1984 by Thomas Nelson Inc. (NKJV); *Holy Bible*, New Living Translation, copyright © 1996. Used by permission of Tyndale House Publishers, Inc., Wheaton, IL 60189. All rights reserved. (NLT); The New Revised Standard Version of the Bible, copyright © 1989 by the Division of Christian Education of the National Council of the Churches of Christ in the United States of America. Used by permission. All rights reserved. (NRSV); and Revised Standard Version of the Bible, copyright © 1946, 1952, 1971, by the Division of Christian Education of the National Council of the Churches of Christ in the U.S.A. Used by permission. (RSV).

Library of Congress Cataloging-in-Publication Data

Library of Congress Cataloging-in-Publication Data
(Revised for vol. 4)
Those preachin' women.
     Vol. 4 is entitled: Those preaching women.
     Contents: [1] Sermons by Black women preachers – v. 2 More sermons by Black women preachers – v. 3 Black Women Preachers Tackle Tough Questions.
1. Sermons, American. 2. Women clergy. I. Mitchell, Ella Pearson
BV4241.T475 1985
25285-4731
ISBN 0-8170-1073-4 (pbk. : v.1)
ISBN 0-8170-1131-5 (v.2)
ISBN 0-8170-1249-4 (v.3)
ISBN 0-8170-1464-0 (v.4)

Printed in the U.S.A.

10 09 08 07 06 05 04

10 9 8 7 6 5 4 3 2 1

To all the sisters in ministry
and to those who
have yet to answer God's call.

Contents

Foreword
by Vashti McKenzie...**ix**

Preface...**xi**

Acknowledgements...**xii**

1 Are You Still Answering God's Call?
by Lois A. Poag-Ray...**1**

2 "Tell Them I'm Child of God"
by Cheryl Townsend Gilkes...**6**

3 It's Time to Break the Silence
by Lisa D. Rhodes...**11**

4 Mustard-Seed Faith
by Diane Givens Moffett...**16**

5 What the Devil Didn't Know
by Bernadette Glover-Williams...**21**

6 Lift and Stretch
by Betty Wright-Riggins...**26**

7 Let Us Prophesy
by Cecelia Williams Bryant...**31**

8 Dance with My Father
by Renita J. Weems...**35**

9 But Grow in Grace
by Lois B. Fortson...**40**

10 Tabitha, Arise; Dorcas, Get Up!
by Cassandra A. Sparrow...**45**

11 The Main Issue
by J. Ruth Travis...**50**

12 A Word for the Weary
by Mary H. Young...**55**

Contents

13 The Declaration of Forgiven Disciples
    *by Lisa Roxanne Harris...***60**

14 The Spiritually Connected Family
    *by Jacqueline E. McCullough...***65**

15 Sisters in the Right Place at the Right Time
    *by Carolyn Tyler Guidry...***70**

16 It's a Good Thing!
    *by Jo Ann Browning...***75**

17 Can Any Good Thing Come out of Nazareth?
    *by Audrey Bronson...***80**

18 A Journey of Blind Faith
    *by Lillie Lawton Travis...***84**

19 From Easter to Epiphany to Eternity
    *by Cheryl D. Ward...***89**

20 The Bridge Across the Gap
    *by Angela Williams...***94**

21 Anointed for This
    *by Leah E. White...***99**

22 When the Manna Ceases
    *by Henrietta Carter...***104**

23 Leah: Rejected but Not Forgotten
    *by Nancy Crawford Sanders...***109**

24 Come Out and Stay Out!
    *by Elaine McCollins Flake...***114**

25 That's Love
    *by Fleeta Turrentine...***118**

About Those Preaching Women...**123**

Foreword

Preaching and the black church are like wet to water. It is hard to imagine one without the other. Preaching is imperative to the worship experience whether it is done in the cane brakes or brush arbors of the South, storefront tabernacles, converted movie house citadels, urban cathedrals, or suburban mega-structures.

The preaching tradition is a strong expression that often defies description and definition. It is an oral synchronization of sight and sound that brings to life dynamically the Word of God. Sometimes it is quiet fire that spreads silently, burning into the hearts of its hearers. It can be a blazing forest fire that brings down tall timbers of resistance to discipleship. It can be a controlled flame that methodically takes its time to reduce the rubbish of hurt and anger and the pain of injustice. It can simmer like smoldering embers, just enough to keep the flame of faith alive in hard times.

Preaching in the black church is an art form of stylized language that speaks, sings, dances, whoops, and rolls through the Old and New Testaments. It is drama that unfolds ancient stories with a relevant hermeneutic from a fertile, creative imagination. This hermeneutic is unique, different from other cultures or ethnic groups.

Preaching is a mixing bowl in which intellect and emotion are stirred together. Head and heart are blended with divine interaction into a potent feast. It is a tool of social justice and spiritual transformation that empowers its hearers. It is a gift given, but at the same time is something that requires prayer, study, preparation, and discipline.

Every preacher has the same textbook: the Bible. Every preacher has the opportunity to utilize scholarly research and references. Yet sermons rarely come out the same way. God speaks through the human vessels that contain heritage and history, education and training, and both experience and experiences.

Assisted by Jacqueline Glass, Dr. Ella P. Mitchell once again provides visibility to women who powerfully present the message of Christ. In this fourth volume of *Those Preaching Women*, our dean of preaching women allows the reader to explore the vast range of prophetic gifts.

These preaching women proclaim messages diverse in presentation and style. They are biblical communicators who bring a fresh perspective with the prophetic flair, representatives of the profound prophecies and the rich heritage of the black hermeneutic. Their pulpit may be in the sanctuary, as is the case for Dr. Leah White. Or the academy, as it is with Dr. Cheryl Townsend Gilkes. Or in missions, the "pulpit" of Dr. Cecelia Williams Bryant. Each preaching woman has her own style and her own way to "say it!" They all "tell it," speaking the truth, challenging the reader without compromising substance for style.

Those Preaching Women IV is a good investment for those who need an encouraging word. It is also ideal for the student who wants to understand and perhaps to emulate effective Christian communicators. This book will help the whole people of God to hear the "still small voice" in this present age. It is also for the woman listening for the text from her context.

Dr. Mitchell is our national treasure—a highly acclaimed preacher who has been the light in the lighthouse for generations of women called to proclaim but with limited access to role models. She consistently presents the voices that need to be heard.

—Bishop Vashti Murphy McKenzie
Presiding Prelate, 18th Episcopal District
African Methodist Episcopal Church

Preface

In the early years of the third millennium, it is no secret that the presence of the female preacher is being felt. She is here to stay. Her presence is evidenced by the swelling numbers of female seminarians graduating from theological schools across the country. It is evidenced in the pulpits of churches across the country led by female pastors. And also by the increasing number of women ministers who are becoming chaplains, associate pastors, and even bishops.

The black church historically has made it difficult for women pursuing a preaching ministry. Because of the many challenges and practical issues women face in ministry, the calling can be described as "uphill." Despite this "uphill" calling on the lives of female clergy—and notwithstanding the many challenges that accompany this call—I am convinced that women will continue to be major instruments of effective change to many congregations in a variety of denominations and church settings across the globe. And they will continue to register their influence on the paradigm of the black church.

No longer is the question, "Should women be allowed to preach?" History has shown us that women were answering the call of God throughout the 19th and 20th centuries: Jareena Lee, Zilpha Elaw, Julia A.J. Foote, and Ella Pearson Mitchell, to name a few. The dedication of ordinary and extraordinary women such as these has helped make the church one of the most stable entities in the black community.

The question for today is, "How can we encourage women to continue answering the call of God and to press on in the name of Jesus?" The contributions of these twenty-five preaching women—who represent diversity with respect to age, geography, and ministerial assignment—constitute an inspiring response to this question.

—Jacqueline B. Glass

Acknowledgements

No book or research is ever completed without the help of a number of people. This is particularly true of a collection of sermons. The persons invited to contribute to this volume are invariably busy professionals. The word they preach comes out of the richness of the experience that feeds each of their ministries. We, the editors, dare not take this for granted. So, first of all, we express our boundless gratitude to our twenty-five contributors for taking time out to share and to do so in the timely fashion required by the publishing process.

Because our authors are so busy, we have had to rely at times on their staffs and assistants. So secondly, we express our gratitude for the very important cooperation of contributors' staffs and assistants, people we rarely had the opportunity to meet in person.

We are honored that Bishop McKenzie accepted the invitation to write the Foreword for this volume. As usual, her words were at once very gracious and full of insight.

When Jackie and I needed some help with editing, we recruited the assistance of my teammate and spouse, Henry. He took time out from his latest book (due to be published in the fall) to contribute to the editing of this volume. We are grateful as well for the constant support of Linda Peavy and Randy Frame of Judson Press.

Finally, what good would a book be without readers? So we extend our warm appreciation to you, the readers, for the support and promotion of this series of books and of the cause of freedom for black women in the pulpit. We hope to reach out with encouragement to a rapidly growing new community of female preachers. This would be impossible without you.

—Ella Pearson Mitchell

Are You Still Answering God's Call?

BY LOIS A. POAG-RAY

Also I heard the voice of the Lord, saying,
Whom shall I send, and who will go for us?
Then said I, Here am I; send me.
(Isaiah 6:8)

It is easy to sit in the comfort zones of our Christianity, doing the same things that we did years ago, using twentieth-century models for twenty-first-century people. We desire a pilgrim's journey that is smooth and unencumbered—no detours, no delays, no surprises, no hardships, nothing new, nothing different, no uninvited persons invading our thoughts with their conversation, distracting us from whatever is on our agendas for that day. But in the real world, at least once a year there comes a time for an annual Christian check-up—accountability time, disclosure time. It could be those forty days of Lent or the Advent season. It could be an annual conference or time for the church's annual report. Whatever the occasion, it is a time that requires us to check hard facts, quantify our service, and qualify our work. Faced with the dilemma of how and with whom we have been traveling this Christian journey, the enduring question to believers of all generations and of all times resounds once again: "Are you still answering God's call?"

Our text reminds us that no matter how we have been traveling—and even when we feel that we have fallen from grace—God is never finished with us. For every believer, there will come a time when God issues a new command, a new summons, a new call. It will be a call to higher service or greater challenges. In the words of the old spiritual, "every round goes higher, higher," because we are "soldiers of the cross!"

The disciple Peter's journey is an excellent example of how God works in the life of the believer. Recall Peter's loyalty and his prophetic acknowledgement of Jesus as "the Christ." Remember Peter's indignation over Jesus' reference to himself as a "suffering servant" and Peter's pledge of undying friendship (see Mark 14:27-30). We know the painful story of Peter's three denials just before the trial and crucifixion when he was asked about his connection to Jesus.

In John 21, we find Peter having returned to his old comfort zone. He remembers his comfort zone so clearly that when it really mattered, he had forgotten about his promises to Jesus. He had forgotten about walking with Jesus on the water and being there when Jesus fed 5,000 people with two fishes and five loaves. And when accountability time had come, when the cock had crowed for the third time, Peter realized that he had done nothing he had promised to do, and he was left with the memory of his failure. But, Jesus was not finished with Peter!

As believers, we must always be ready to receive and to answer God's new call. The great German theologian Dietrich Bonhoeffer reminds us of the cost of discipleship, asserting that there is no such thing as "cheap grace." He suggests to us that when the call comes to a person, it comes to that person alone, and that God's call will come more than once. It will not be your brother's call or your sister's call; it's *your* call. It's not just a call for preachers or evangelists or missionaries. It's a call for anyone and everyone who claims to know and love the Lord Jesus. Moreover, it's not just a one-time call to discipleship. It's a second and then a third call to service. Sometimes it's a get-ready call, because our spiritual foundation needs strengthening in preparation for another level of service. Sometimes it's a recall, taking us back to the basics of our love connection with God. Sometimes it's a wake-up call, because we fell asleep on God and his work. But whatever it is, the call will come.

In these early years of a new millennium, God is issuing a wake-up call for the Church. Strange voices and strange cults are leading our people astray. They hunger and thirst for God's Word but are fed a diet of political correctness and pomp and circumstance. Our young and old have lost sight of meaningful and purposeful living. It is time for the Church to hear the age-old cry, "Whom shall I send? Who will go for us?" and to sound the right response: "Here am I, Lord. Send me!"

John 21 highlights at least three realities of God's call and our response. First, God's call will always come at the right time, in the right place, and for the right task. Notice that by the time of this encounter with Jesus, Peter had been in Jesus' presence on at least three other post-resurrection occasions. However, it was only at that particular time, at that particular place, that Jesus issued that particular call on the disciple's life.

It was then, after Peter and the other disciples had experienced their shame and their emptiness, after they had realized the need for direction in their lives, after they had returned to business as usual, but found no joy in the old ways. It was there at the seashore, after they had caught such an abundance of fish that their nets could not hold the catch, that Jesus appealed to his disciples with new instructions. And only then, after they had dined, did Jesus focus his attention on Peter and call him by name: not "Peter" the strong, stable rock of a man, but "Simon, son of Jonas." It matters little when, or where, or even how we expect God's call to come. Simply be assured that the call will come, but always in God's own time, at God's appointed place, and with God's chosen task for you. Regardless of the time, place, or task, our answer should be, "Yes, Lord."

Secondly, God's call is always accompanied by an attitude of humility—even a feeling of unworthiness. Yes, God wants us to be bold, unafraid, and confident. However, God also wants us to walk humbly with him (see Micah 6:8). The world teaches us to exalt ourselves, to blow our own horns, and even to flaunt our sins and our treachery. But it is our attitude that reflects with whom we are walking and whose summons we are answering.

Consider Jesus' temptation in the wilderness, and be aware that when Satan tempts us, it is always with an appeal to our pride, our arrogance, or our desire to satisfy the flesh. However, God's call is never about self; rather, it is about being a blessing to someone else. It is never about our glory, but God's glory. In this "me" generation, it is not about praise to us; it is about praise to God who created, saved, and nurtured us.

We need more Isaiahs who will cry, "Woe is me." We need more Peters who will weep in utter shame when they realize that they, too, have failed and faltered and deserted Christ. We need more Pauls who will acknowledge their sinfulness: "Oh wretched man that I am; what I would do, that do I not; but what I hate, that I do" (Romans 7:15,24).

God told Paul that he needed to put aside his pride and his concern about some affliction because of the sufficiency of God's grace. God instructed Isaiah not to worry, because he would touch his lips and "your iniquity [will be] taken away, and your sin purged" (Isaiah 6:7, NKJV). "Don't worry, Peter," said the Lord. "I have forgiven you and restored you, and I'll breathe on you so that you will walk in new power!" Each of those men answered God's call. They humbled themselves, and they worked miracles because they understood that God's power works more effectively through an attitude of humility. And the question resounds: "Are you still answering God's call?"

Thirdly, if you love the Lord, the call will always lead to action. Examine the first time Jesus asked Peter the question, "Do you truly love me more than these?" (John 21:15, NIV). Perhaps the reference here was to the pull of all that Peter had left behind or to Peter's love for earthly gain. Perhaps Jesus was referring to the comfort zone that we mortals tend to create for ourselves. Whatever the case, Jesus wants to know whether or not we love him more than all these other things.

The second time Jesus simply asked, "Do you truly love me?" (21:16, NIV). Too often, the significance of these "love" questions is missed because we overlook the fact that the English language has only one word to describe the many nuances of love. However, in the Greek text, the first two times the "love" question is asked, Jesus uses the Greek word *agapao* or *agape* love—that deeply unconditional, sacrificial, divine love. But Peter's response, "Lord, you know that I love you" (21:15, 16, NIV), used another word for "love"—*phileo*, which is brotherly love or friendly love. It is still love, although a lesser degree of it and not as noble or as abundant as *agape* love. When Jesus asked the "love" question for the third time, he used that lesser word for love. It is as though Jesus were saying to Peter, "I know that you love me, even if that love is not as complete as you think it should be."

4

Three times Peter had denied Christ, and now three times he had affirmed his love for Jesus, but using this lesser word for love: "Lord, you know all things (Lord, you know my heart, my attitudes, my fears, my strengths, my weaknesses, my failures); you know that I love you" (21:17, NIV). Acknowledging one more time a confessional statement from Peter, Jesus issued this new call: "Feed my sheep" (21:18, NIV). And Peter went to work. With the disciples in that upper room, in the temple, at Pentecost, in the church, with Cornelius and his family, and in the jail, Peter did the work of spreading the good news of Jesus Christ. Peter's love for Christ, flawed as it was, led him to action.

In the final analysis, beloved, when we consider our personal journeys, it is clear that God can take our "little bit of love," just as he takes our "little bit of faith," and can work miracles in our lives and in the lives of those whom we touch. And in the midst of our humility and feelings of unworthiness, and in the midst of our concerns about the right time and the right place, and in the midst of our reluctance to step out of the boxes of our lives, God still calls to us, "Whom shall I send, who will go for us?" And through our love for God, we give the only possible answer, "Here am I, Lord. Send me!"

Beloved, are you still answering God's call? Let your answer be in the affirmative: "Yes, Lord, I'm still answering your call."

"Tell Them I'm a Child of God"

BY CHERYL TOWNSEND GILKES

Of what people art thou? . . . I am an Hebrew;
and I fear the LORD, the God of heaven, which hath
made the sea and the dry land.
(Jonah 1:8-9)

The call to God's service is one of the most important and powerful events in a Christian's life, irrespective of the level of service and regardless of our struggle with such an experience—how quickly or slowly we answer God's call and embrace God's will for our lives. In the end we learn that we serve a God who takes not only the best within us but also our faults, our failures, our needs—all of our humanness—and consecrates them to his service. God makes the particularities of our lives a part of that universal blessing of humanity—part of the "all things" so celebrated by Paul as working together for good for them who love the Lord and are called according to his purpose (see Romans 8:28).

The story of Jonah is an important lesson about God's understanding of us. The call to any Christian service challenges each and every one of us, like Jonah, to think about who we are in the world and who we are in relation to the various human communities that constitute our world. For Jonah, the crisis comes when he flees from God's call to minister to Nineveh, an historic enemy of God's people, Israel. Fleeing in the opposite direction, Jonah gets on a boat, hides in the very bottom and tries to sleep his way through the storm that descends on them. The multi-

6

national (and therefore interfaith) membership of the crew knows that this is an out-of-season storm and seeks to discern whose deity is angry with whom. Having exhausted all of their methods of divination, they awaken Jonah, the only person whose deity and nation remain to be accounted for.

"Are you the reason that this storm has descended upon us?" "Who are you?" "What is your occupation?" "What are your origins?" "What are your roots?" "Who are your people?" Then there is the most fundamental question of all: "Of which people art thou?" Or, more precisely in the ancient near-eastern imagination, "Who is your god?"

These are familiar questions for those of us who have grown up black in America. "Who are your people?" is the question we often hear when we behave in ways that are puzzling to other folks. "What are you?" is the question often asked when our color does not quite place us in absolute, unquestionable categories. "What do you do?" and "Where did you go to school?" are the questions that seek to probe our position in the class continuum. "What church do you go to?" and "Who's your pastor?" are the questions that try to identify our religious affiliation.

Often the interrogators become very frustrated when we respond, "Who wants to know?" "Why does it matter?" "What's the big deal?" "What's it to you anyhow?" "Why you askin'?" "Whatchulookinat?" We answer this way because often the questions about "what" we are objectify us in a world where human social location becomes a matter of life and death—sometimes in the immediacy of war, peace, and violent human conflict and sometimes in the long-run of life, of chances and exclusions.

Our ancestors understood these questions of objectification and dehumanization. In their wisdom, honed in the fires of the slave community, they understood what it was to be called out of their names, to be considered less than human, to be forced to be breeders and beasts of burden, to bear the lash, and to be called "everything but a child of God." These people sang an old spiritual that Jonah helps us to remember today: "If anybody asks you who I am . . . tell them I'm a child of God."

In this society, our lives are fragmented and compartmentalized. Our religious identity, our faith, is just one hat of many hats that we wear—

class, race, ethnicity, marital status, parental status. Religion becomes a hat to be worn only in the religious hat shop. When the scene changes, our hats should change. If we don't change our hats, we are seen as unsophisticated and unready to participate fully and intelligently in this modern, secularized society. Our failure to wear the appropriate hat in the appropriate place is a sign of personal disorganization. But I hear the ancestors saying, "Ain't gonna lay my 'ligion down!"

Additionally, in our well-compartmentalized and appropriately fragmented world, our religion, our denominational affiliation, and our style of spirituality become indications of our modernity. Is our worship service too long? Is the music too loud? Will we have to choose between the boss's brunch or communion service? Sunday service becomes a mere rest stop in the weekly round of activities, and we have drive-in churches where we receive spiritual fast food, short-order bread of heaven, and special-order waters of salvation, the kinds that don't upset us.

Or better yet, we can watch church on the widescreen television and hear that it is patriotic to look down on the poor, that it is OK to demand material blessings from God, and that the sick are sick because they lack faith. Poverty, injustice, malnutrition, AIDS, welfare, and Medicaid are symptoms of a lack of faith, a lack of personal responsibility—on the part of the widows, the orphans, the homeless, the fatherless. If you tune in and partner up you will never have to leave your home to see the homeless sleeping in doorways and begging on the streets. In our neat and well-ordered, compartmentalized world where religion has its place—not too big a place—we will never have to wonder if one of "the least of these" (Matthew 25:40) whom we pass on the street is actually Jesus in disguise challenging us to live our faith fully in an unjust world.

Jonah's world, however, was not compartmentalized and well-ordered. Faith and allegiance to one's deity could not be separated from other aspects of life. In the midst of this storm, in the midst of the life-threatening crisis facing this ship—this multi-national life-world, a world that was reeling and rocking, a world where everyone faced disaster and destruction together—Jonah had only one answer to the multiple questions being asked: "I am an Hebrew; and I fear the LORD, the God of heaven, which hath made the sea and the dry land" (Jonah 1:9).

Jonah is forced to answer, and in answering he is forced to testify: "I come from a people who were delivered by the most powerful God, the most high God, the only true and living God, the Lord our God who is one God. I come from a people who serve the God of Hosts, God Almighty, the King of Glory, the Most High God. I am an Hebrew. I serve the Lord, the God of Abraham, Isaac, and Jacob. My society is a sacred society. Every day, every hour, my people call upon the Lord."

I can hear Jonah now: "We must know the Lord. We must walk with the Lord and remind one another that the Lord our God is one God. We love the Lord with all our hearts and with all our souls and with all our might. We must teach this diligently to our children. We must talk about this when we are sitting in our houses, when we are walking down the road, when we lay down in the evening, and when we rise up in the morning. We bind the great commandments of our Lord on our hands and we hang them between our eyes and we write the great words of God on our doorposts. We live our lives so that we can never forget that the Lord our God is one God and God has brought us from a mighty long way."

"And of which people art thou?" What is *our* answer today? The life of God's people is bound up in being able to give an account of ourselves when the storms of life are raging. We must have a testimony. We must have a hope. We must have a vision that sees beyond the evils of the moment and bears witness to our God. In spite of the fragmented ways we may be questioned and challenged about who and what we are, and in spite of the scattered way in which we live our lives and develop our persons, our faith, our spirituality, there is for us like there was for Jonah one all-encompassing answer: "I am a child of God."

No matter how far Jonah tried to run away from God, Jonah could not forget where he came from. In our prosperity and upward mobility, we cannot forget about the grandmothers who bore witness to their faith while working in Miss Anne's kitchens and the grandfathers who raised the hymns on Sunday after bearing burdens and disrespect all week long. We cannot forget the songs about salvation and transformation that have come "Since I Met Jesus." We cannot forget about deacons and missionaries who led prayer meetings, or about ushers and church mothers who shouted "Thank you, Jesus!" whenever the Holy Ghost stopped by. And we cannot forget that it was often the poorest sister who worked the longest hours in somebody's kitchen who was the one with the longest testimony, the best songs, and the most money raised every Women's Day. We cannot forget the folks whose songs, prayers, sermons, and testimonies moved us to hear the good news of Jesus. And when someone challenges our beings and our persons and our humanity and calls us everything but a child of God, then our souls must sing, "Take me back . . . where I first received You . . . where I first believed."

If anybody asks you who I am, please tell them I'm a child of God. I am somebody who comes from a people that the Lord came down to deliver from slavery. I am somebody whose bloodlines run deep through the hush harbors of this nation's hard and bloody history of slavery. I am somebody whose bloodlines run back across an ocean floor strewn with the bones of the Middle Passage. I am somebody whose bloodlines run deep through the good earth of West and Central Africa, whose bloodlines run east to a land the prophets called Cush, whose bloodlines turn north and run back twenty centuries to a place called Calvary beneath the cross of Jesus. If anybody asks you who I am, tell them that "there is a fountain filled with blood drawn from Emmanuel's veins." If anybody asks you who I am, please tell them I'm a child of God.

It's Time to Break
the Silence

BY LISA D. RHODES

For if you keep silence at such a time as this,
relief and deliverance will rise for the Jews from another quarter,
but you and your father's family will perish.
Who knows? Perhaps you have come to royal dignity
for such a time as this.
(Esther 4:14, NRSV)

Esther, one of two books in the Bible named after a woman, begins with Queen Vashti's refusal to obey a summons from her husband, King Ahasuerus. In this time, women were expected to obey the commands of their husbands. Vashti, the Persian queen who was living in opulence, is cast out of the kingdom for refusing to come to a celebrative feast at the king's command. She loses her crown, her social and political status, and all the privileges associated with her royalty.

Queen Vashti's refusal to display her beauty like a show piece and lose what dignity and integrity she had left put her in an awkward position: "No, I refuse to be exploited by you parading me in front of your boys. No, I refuse to allow you to ill-define me, and through me, the many women whose dignity and respect I represent." Perhaps Vashti, like many women then and now, had one too many disrespectful and insensitive demands placed upon her. I imagine, like Fannie Lou Hamer, the passionate civil rights worker, Vashti "was sick and tired of being sick and tired." And so, as one of the first woman activists portrayed in ancient

11

culture, Queen Vashti decided to honor her inner voice and take a stand, step out, and speak on behalf of a woman's right to say "no."

Without a Vashti there would not be a Queen Esther. Just as there would not be an Angela Davis without a Harriet Tubman; or a Maya Angelou without a Phyllis Wheatley; or a Vashti McKenzie without a Jarena Lee. Queen Vashti stood up and prepared the way for Esther, who, like many of us, grew up in the church. But when her Uncle Mordecai, one of the many Jews taken into Babylonian captivity, decided to have Esther enter "star search," a Persian pageant designed to replace Queen Vashti, Esther was instructed to keep her Jewish identity, and therein her cultural and religious heritage, a real secret.

Esther was asked by her cousin Mordecai—the one who loved her and raised her after the death of her parents, the one who cared for her well-being and nurtured her faith, the one who taught her how to pray three times a day—to please hide her Jewish identity. Mordecai wanted the best for Esther. He wanted her to fit in and be accepted by the Babylonian elite, to be trained in Babylonian arts and culture and educated in the finest of Babylonian schools.

Esther assimilated and hid her identity well, and for so long she denied the laws and customs that governed the Jewish people. So when Mordecai asked for help to save their people, Esther forgot who she was. She had adopted the Babylonian hairstyle, adorned herself with clothes from Babylonian designers, communicated in the king's language, and focused on pleasing the king rather than on pleasing the God who had delivered her people out of Egypt.

Esther forgot who she was and was trying desperately to be somebody she was not. She forgot that she was a carrier of the promise given by the God of Israel through Sarah. She forgot that she was a descendant of the survivors of the Exodus and an offspring of the Joshua generation. The farther Esther walked away from her Jewish identity, the smaller Hadassah became. Esther forgot that she was Hadassah, taken from Jerusalem with her uncle and now living in exile.

So when Mordecai learned of the Persian prime minister Haman's plan to destroy all the Jews because Mordecai did not bow down to him, Mordecai tore off his clothes, put on sackcloth and ashes, ran out into the middle of Susa, the capital city of Persia, as far out as the law would allow, and mourned violently in the streets. We learn in the text that Mordecai was desperately seeking a way to save his people. Through Hatach, Esther's attendant, Mordecai urged Esther to go into the king's presence to beg for mercy and plead with him on behalf of the Jews. But when you forget who you are and want to distance yourself from where you came from, you become silent on social and political issues that will adversely impact your present and future life.

Initially Esther hesitated to give way to her secret. For breaking secrets can mean personal exposure, ridicule, and rejection. Young girls who are molested by family members, altar boys who are molested by priests, or women who are abused by spouses have extreme difficulty giving voice to their silent pain and suffering. Family members who have lost loved ones or experienced delays in their ability to give voice to their grief struggle. The patient man, Job, struggled for seven days before giving voice to his grief over the loss of his children, possessions, and health. It took Maya Angelou several years after being raped to break her silence and talk. Homosexual and gay men and women and AIDS victims struggle with breaking the silence for fear of losing their jobs, their public offices, or their credibility.

Esther did not want to break the silence about her Jewish identity, for it would have meant sacrificing the royal crown and possibly her life. But if she did not, it would mean the destruction of all the Jews, young and old, women and children, in one day. Women have always had difficult choices to make between personal freedom and financial security, self preservation and the survival of their families, community and their people. What would you choose? Vashti chose personal freedom for all the Jews, at the expense of giving up all the splendor of the Persian kingdom.

Why did Vashti choose to give it all up? Well, feminist theologians, women who seek to understand God and want to interpret Scripture from the perspective of gender equality and justice, would say that it was time. It was time to break the silence and challenge the systems, structures, norms, traditions, and laws that defined women but excluded their contributions to family, culture, and history. They would say that it was time, time to break the silence and speak to the subordinate role of women and honor the "sacred feminine" in us all.

Womanist theologians would add to a feminist perspective the unique experiences of black women—our mothers, grandmothers, and great-grandmothers of the African Diaspora. These were women whose voices were muzzled, women who might have been but were not allowed to be, so they died with their "springs of creativity" stifled and with unborn contributions within them.

Vashti chose to stand up and break the silence of her oppression. As a woman, what will you choose? What would Esther choose? All Esther could hear in her head was Mordecai saying, "For if you keep [silent, for if you keep silent, for if you keep silent,] at such a time as this, relief and deliverance will rise for the Jews from another quarter, but you and your father's family will perish. Who knows? Perhaps you have come to royal dignity for such a time as this" (4:14, NRSV).

Sisters and brothers, we have been silent for too long. We have closed the doors to our emotional pain and suffering, and we will not say a word. We continue to accept broken hearts because of our desire to keep a man or a woman close. Therefore, we say nothing about the interpersonal injustices, infidelity, and abuse. We continue to endure the escalating devastation in our communities, the alarming rates of divorce, teenage pregnancy, poor test scores, and low achievement, because we do not speak up on issues that are related to educational reform and multicultural curriculum development. We are losing the trust and respect of young black America because we are not willing to give voice to our own anxieties about the hip-hop generation and its revolutionary message.

We have been silent on issues related to black male/female relationships, silent on issues related to the civil and human rights of homosexual men and women. We have been silent on issues of sexuality and the black church, while AIDS is killing young black America in disproportionate numbers. We have been silent on women in the church and the ordination of women, when over seventy-five percent of most church memberships are made up of women.

It's time to break the silence. Do not let fear of losing privilege, becoming vulnerable or exposed, hinder you from breaking the silence. Give voice to the injustices in your personal space, workplace, community, church, and the world. Break the silence.

Esther's second reply to Mordecai was, "[After I fast] for three days, night or day . . . I will go to the king, though it is against the law; and if I perish, I perish" (4:16, NRSV). God was working in Esther. She grabbed hold of her faith, fell to her knees, and asked God for fearless courage to do the work that God had called her to do. You too, on faith, can break the silence and carry with you the truth of who you are.

There will always come a time when the silence must be broken and the truth must be told; a time when some poor alcoholic will fall down and say, "My life has become unmanageable"; a time when a mother and father must tell their children they are getting a divorce; a time when a teenage girl must tell her parents she is having a baby; a time when a son must tell his parents that he has AIDS; a time when a husband must tell his wife that he has been unfaithful. There will always come a time when women must stand up to be heard; a time when a people must fight for their lives and strive to be free; a time when a slave must call out, "Freedom, freedom, before I'd be a slave, I'll be buried in my grave and go home to be with Jesus and be free." There will always come a time when a Sojourner Truth must stand to proclaim the rights of women; a time when a Richard Allen must break away and start a new thing—the A.M.E. church; a time when a Rosa Parks must sit down and a Martin Luther King Jr. must stand up; a time when the everlasting God must step out into the Garden of Eden and call out to man and woman, "Where are thou?" (Genesis 3:9). Like it was for Vashti, who had to make a choice, it is time to break the silence.

Mustard-Seed Faith

BY DIANE GIVENS MOFFETT

*And the Lord said, "If ye had faith as a grain
of mustard seed, ye might say unto this sycamine tree,
Be thou plucked up by the root, and be thou planted
in the sea; and it should obey you."*
(Luke 17:6)

As a part of our New Year's celebration, my mother would host gatherings for our extended family in which everyone came to our home and shared a hearty meal that included a wide variety of delicious, meticulously prepared foods. One of those foods that I personally did not like was "chitterlings," or "chittlins." Chittlins are what our African slave ancestors prepared when they had nothing else to eat. The odor of cooking chittlins was so terrible that they had to be cooked outdoors—otherwise the smell penetrated every nook and cranny of the house and stayed there.

I never dreamed there was anything in common between chittlins and mustard seeds, but then I read John Crossan's book, *Jesus: A Revolutionary Biography*. In this book I learned a whole new angle on the meaning of Jesus' parable of the mustard seed. I learned that a mustard seed, once it has been sown, is almost impossible to get rid of. The seed germinates at once and becomes an immediate threat to the whole garden. Even when it was domesticated, farmers had to take action to curb its growth. If it was left to grow freely in a grain field, a mustard plant could destroy the whole crop. So *that's* why it's like chittlins! The odor of cooking chittlins could drown out all the savory odors of Mom's finest delicacies, so she had to cook the chittlins outdoors. And farmers had to

16

grow mustard plants separately from the other crops, or they would choke out all the more desirable plants.

Jesus is not talking about a comparably undesirable faith, but he is helping us envision a faith that covers and coats the way we think, the way we speak, and the way we act. He is talking about faith that permeates our minds and saturates our souls. He is talking about faith that makes a difference in our outlook and attitude on every single aspect of life. He is talking about a faith that, once planted, will increase, covering everything we think and say and do.

I always thought the mustard seed symbolized the great growth of the kingdom and the blessings that could come to us if we only had a little bit of real faith. That is still true, but grain farmers in Jesus' day would probably have had a different take. You see, they were particularly cautious of a mustard plant, because it could become so large that nesting birds would make a home in the plant and cause permanent threat to the other seed and grain. And those lovely birds could be very destructive. In light of this, the point of Jesus' parable was not so much the size of the proverbially tiny seed, but rather that it tends to take over where it is not invited, attracting undesirable birds and causing damage. The faith that parallels the mustard seed starts out small and begins to seep into every aspect of our beings, coloring our personalities and transforming our lives.

How do we get mustard-seed faith? I am convinced that one of the reasons the disciples asked Jesus to increase their faith was that they could see the power inherent in believing and trusting. They could see that in and through Jesus' ministry, faith was effective. They saw him heal a woman who had had a hemorrhage for twelve years. They saw him liberate a lady who'd been bent over for sixteen years. They wanted increased faith to deal with the challenges of life in an effectual manner. And we want likewise!

We realize that our faith is not where we want it to be. Our faith is too limited and confined; it rises in the sanctuary but dissipates in the ordinary. It is stirred up when we come to worship but locked up when we go to work. It peaks in times of joy, but it plummets in times of adversity. How do we get faith to increase?

One important way to grow in faith is the way the disciples did: to spend more time with Jesus and people of faith. The disciples saw faith in the woman with an issue of blood, as she reached out and touched the hem of Jesus' garment. They saw it when the woman who had been bent over and pressed down for sixteen years came to Jesus, so they wanted their own faith increased. Their request was already being granted by their just being with Jesus as he worked. In other words, to grow in faith, spend a lot of time around it. Faith is contagious. It is much more caught than taught.

This is how our ancestors received faith and passed it on, even in the midst of the degrading and devastating institution of slavery. Mustard-seed faith was caught by contagion, as civil rights workers marched and sang their hearts out. Many a young agnostic became a believer after marching shoulder-to-shoulder with believers at places like Selma and Montgomery.

Another way to receive increased faith is to employ one's own mind in thinking the thoughts of faith. The Book of Hebrews declares that, "Faith is the substance of things hoped for, the evidence of things not seen" (Hebrews 11:1)—possibilities not yet fulfilled. People with mustard-seed faith have a unique way of thinking; the seed of faith invades their mental mode. In other words, mustard-seed faith is found in the exercise of the mind.

As my daughter Jessica was preparing for a vocal performance, I listened to Mondre, my husband, coaching her. He told her to visualize the sound before she sang the note. He was asking her to see where the tone should be placed, to hear the intonation and color of the note. When she took his direction, the notes flowed flawlessly, ringing with resonance! She had begun to think differently. Those seeking faith visualize possibilities, which brings us to another facet: seeing in the mind. One needs it especially in self-perception—self-esteem.

After all our fighting to eradicate slavery and enforce civil rights, few were dealing with healing our low self-esteem, an evil byproduct of racism. We still think that "white is right." And too many of us still think that straight hair is better than curly hair. We still think our counterparts' culture and style of worship are better than ours. We don't realize that imitation is a failure of faith in our Creator. Some black churches are dull and empty of spiritual vitality, trying to be something we are not. When we see ourselves as born handicapped, we see God as unjust. When we habitually envision ourselves as beautiful, black, and lovely, we are prone to grow in the faith, because that's how God made us. It heals our self-esteem and brings new spiritual strength and faith. Faith in the mind reaches limits. We need to put faith into action, which can be done by expressing faith in word and deed.

Not only does mustard-seed faith grow in the mind; it also grows in the mouth. When we express our faith, we grow in faith. We get on record, and we are motivated to live up to it. When Jesus said, "I am," his in-mind faith was presented as faith in his mouth.

Our faith grows when we say to others, "I am able to do what God has called me to do. I can change what God has called me to change. I am able, not because I am better than someone else, but because God is working in me." We can meet family needs, deal with a disease, and live without a spouse or a significant other. We can have joy in the midst of sorrow. We can help others accomplish goals. We can work it—whatever it is—because we have said so in faith.

Yes, faith grows in the mouths of people who understand their identity and witness to God's will for their lives. Want to increase your faith? Try openly affirming what God has already done in and through you, not out of arrogance or conceit, but in thanks for God's goodness.

Mustard-seed faith grows through contact with people of faith, in the mind, and in the mouth, and, finally, it grows in our mannerisms. Mannerisms need to be dealt with, because they are unconsciously testifying to others. A perpetual frown says a lot about our faith, and so does a gracious smile. We need to be sure our body language—our mannerisms—are consistent with our faith.

Habits of manner are built through years of experience. We don't have gracious habits of compassion for people if our case history is one of tight-jawed mannerisms and self-centered concern. We grow in faith when we stay cool and intelligent in a traffic crisis. If our mannerisms in traffic include road rage, it's because we are insecure and untrusting. We can grow in that glorious gift called faith when we start to work at politely chatting with the other driver. Others will know we are Christians by our manners.

Within the community of faith, we witness with mind, mouth, and mannerisms. These are all important to our desire to grow a mustard-seed type of faith. Of course, our faith may not grow as fast as a mustard seed, but by the help of God, it can become as pervasive. Just as the odor of chittlins found every nook and cranny in our old home, we can have a faith that doesn't miss any part of our being. And just as those old mustard plants just grew and grew, so may our personal faith just grow and grow.

As I look at the disciples, I realize that faith made a world of difference in that motley crew, and it didn't happen overnight. I wouldn't have picked such a bunch if I had been Jesus, but when I read of how they launched the gospel to all the world, I have to recognize that, like the mustard plant, they just grew and grew and grew.

I have come to feel the same way about myself. Following my own admonition, I can witness to how far I have grown and say, "I am a child of the Most High God. I am who God wants me to be, and I am very happy about it." The winds of adversity, hardship, and pain may bend me, but they won't break me. I can feel God's power in my still, black soul.

What the Devil Didn't Know

BY BERNADETTE GLOVER-WILLIAMS

But Paul . . . turned and said to the spirit,
I command thee in the name of Jesus Christ to come out of her.
And he came out the same hour.
(Acts 16:18)

Even the most skilled, seasoned strategist can make a mistake. We already witnessed the war with Iraq. Our country's top leaders came up with a plan with a timeline. And now that the timeline has expired, we all realize that although our leaders were seasoned and skilled, they made a mistake. In the same way, Satan may be crafty, and he may know a lot, but he doesn't know everything. God knows everything, but the devil doesn't know everything. Even though Satan is skilled, and even though he has been extremely effective and efficient ever since the Garden of Eden, he did not realize that in Philippi three of his favorite tactics would backfire.

In Acts 16:16-22, the devil underestimated Paul and his team. And the same tactics that the enemy tried in Philippi, he's trying right now. He's trying them in New Jersey, trying them in Virginia, trying them nationwide right now. So, what can we learn from this text? Three tactics of the enemy: embarrassment, affirmation, and retaliation.

The Bible says in verse 16 of chapter 16 that Paul and his company were on their way to the place of prayer, and they were met by a slave girl who had a spirit of divination—a spirit by which she predicted the future. I have one question. My question is, Whose child was this girl? This slave girl was somebody's baby, yet no one was doing anything to help her. We treat people like her the same way today. Instead of getting help, we just wring our hands and shake our heads and say, "I just don't know what to do." Why not? We shake our heads, suck our teeth, and say, "Isn't it a shame? I don't know what happened." Why don't we object to the exploitation of the vulnerable in our midst? Why don't we defend them against the circus hounds of the world?

You know why? We're embarrassed! We're embarrassed because that is *our* child. We're scared that somebody will look at our child acting out of his natural mind and remember that he is genetically connected to us. We're scared that they will wonder what our problem is too. We think, *Everybody knows I don't have a problem. Everybody knows I'm widely respected in the community. Everybody knows I have more degrees than a thermometer. Everybody knows that I'm in charge of a sorority. Everybody knows I'm a mover and shaker. How could anything like that possibly be related to me?* And so we hide the vulnerable. We hide them. If we let them come to church, we make them sit in the last row, and we bring them in after the service is well underway and kick them out as soon as church is over so nobody can make contact with our "embarrassments."

One of the devil's choice ways of taking over our lives is this tactic of embarrassment. If the enemy can just get you to be embarrassed, you'll never go to rehab. If he can embarrass you, you will do nothing but hide that which is in need of the touch that only God can give. Many of us are sick, yet we die without the help we need. We die in isolation because those who love us love saving their faces more than they love our freedom and healing.

Some churches are a joke of hell. Hell is laughing at many sincere believers who have power when on their knees but do nothing to wage war when they get off their knees. But what the devil did not know in our story, oh, my, the devil did not know that Paul and Silas couldn't have cared less. They couldn't have cared less about looking grand in the eyes of the community. All they knew was that there was a slave girl who was oppressed by a demonic stronghold and needed to be freed. They couldn't have cared less that the church, the place of prayer, had been inspiring on their knees but impotent when they got up off their knees. Paul and Silas refused to be embarrassed by the passivity of the church.

Second tactic. This slave girl kept following behind Paul and his team shouting out, "These men are servants of the most high God and they are telling us the way to be saved" (Acts 16:17, NIV). I've got a question. My question is this: It would seem to me that, through the slave girl, the enemy was affirming Paul's ministry. That wouldn't be annoying to me. But the Bible says that after many days, Paul got sick and tired. Paul was troubled; Paul got annoyed; Paul's last nerve was struck. He turned around, looked at the girl, and said, "In the name of Jesus Christ I command you to come out" (16:18, NIV).

Why did Paul get upset? Paul got upset because he understood that one of the enemy's choice tactics was affirmation. Let me put it like this: We are least scrutinizing, least critical, of the people whom we believe support us. The folk who really know who I am and appreciate me, they're the ones I don't worry about. Oh, let me tell you, it is possible to be seduced by affirmation. It is possible to be seduced into silence and stillness by affirmation that is really coming from the wrong lips. Paul understood that what was coming from this girl was not a declaration of affirmation; it was a tactic designed to distract him from his assignment. It was a tactic designed to massage his ego so that he would no longer remember the fact that here was a life that had been bound and imprisoned and needed to be set free. Paul understood that in spite of the slave girl's glowing words, this was really a manipulative tactic.

The devil didn't realize that manipulation doesn't work on people you want to control when they don't place a value on what you have to offer. In order for you to manipulate me, I have to place a value on—I have to want—what you're offering. Manipulation doesn't work on people who know that they already have access to what you're offering.

The devil offers fortune telling, palm reading, soothsaying, witchcraft— the possibility of reducing anxiety about tomorrow because I can find out what's in tomorrow and plan for it. I got news for you. Because I am a blood-bought child of God, because the one who holds tomorrow is my God and he still sits high and looks low, I don't need you to read my palm.

I don't need you to try to help me manage my world. God's got the whole world and my life in his hands. David said, "The LORD is my light and my salvation; whom shall I fear?" (Psalm 27:1). I don't need you to tell me my future; I know my future. I've got the Holy Spirit; discernment about tomorrow is already at my immediate disposal. I don't need you.

The devil also didn't know that even the final tactic, retaliation, doesn't work. The Bible says in verse 19 of this chapter that when the owners of the slave girl realized that their hope of making money was gone, they seized Paul and Silas and dragged them into the marketplace, where they ended up being stripped and beaten. What the enemy didn't realize was that instead of deactivating the movement of the Holy Spirit by retaliating against Paul and Silas, the girl's owners motivated and fanned the flame of the Holy Spirit. In fact, the retaliation legitimized the miracle in the eyes of everybody who witnessed it.

Why do I say that? The Bible says that the girl's owners filed a complaint with the authorities and told them, "We are now out of business. We are out of business for sure because this girl has been set free." In other words, the owners' complaint is actually a testimony to the power of God. So if anybody in Philippi was wondering if the power of God was real, all they had to do was hear that report. The owners looked at the girl whom they had exploited and realized there was no more money over there. This girl had been changed for good. She would never, ever be the same girl. Their complaint became a testimony that the power of God in the name of Jesus is sufficient to unearth deposits of the demonic that are in the lives of men and women. Their testimony told the whole world that the power of God in the name of Jesus was sufficient to break oppression. Their complaint became a testimony that Jesus seeks to save and to deliver everybody.

And in case no one has told you recently, let me remind you that Jesus Christ is an equal-opportunity liberator. He is an equal-opportunity Savior. He wants the white-collar, the blue-collar, the no-collar, the men, the women, the slaves, the free, the poor, the rich, the middle-class. God wants everybody!

One summer I was walking on the boardwalk in Asbury Park, New Jersey, a shore town that sits right on the Atlantic Ocean. I noticed something—a small store. On it, in big letters, a sign said, "Madam Marie's House of Knowledge." There was this great big eyeball on it—a great big eyeball on "Madam Marie's House of Knowledge." Then I noticed that the place was boarded up. If Madam Marie really knew how to tell the future she would know that she was out of business.

Jesus is real! Yes, he is. And his blood still has enough power to deliver your soul, to save your life, to heal your body and your mind. Every knee, including Madam Marie's knee, shall bow, and every tongue will confess that Jesus Christ is Lord to the glory of the Father (see Isaiah 45:23). The devil doesn't know it, but his days are numbered. I don't care what it looks like, what it feels like, what it sounds like; the forces of evil are doomed. And those who belong to Jesus have access to the very power of God. With God's power, every expression of hell is ultimately defeated through the bloody name of Jesus—Ancient of Days! Hallelujah!

Lift and Stretch

BY BETTY WRIGHT-RIGGINS

And the LORD said unto Moses . . .
Speak unto the children of Israel, that they go forward.
(Exodus 14:15)

There's a story of freedom and emancipation told in the book of Exodus. Some might say it is *"the* story." It is a story of how Yahweh God fashioned a people—how Yahweh called a people, prepared them, chastised them, loved them, and freed them from the bonds of oppression.

You remember the story. Israel was enslaved by the Egyptians. They were burdened and losing hope. They cried out to Yahweh to set them free. You recall how God chose Moses, called and sent him to Pharaoh, demanding that the people go free. After God-guided tests of will and might, Israel walked free from Pharaoh's grasp.

Can you see them? There were over 600,000 people running, skipping, dancing, singing jubilant and joyful. Yahweh God had kept his promise. Israel was excited, obedient, and awed by the wondrous ways of a mighty God. Out there in the wilderness they engaged in sacred rituals to commemorate the passing over of the death angel, sparing their firstborn and taking Pharaoh's own. Every command of God they obeyed. Every direction given to them by Moses they followed. Onward they went. Not knowing where, but assured that God was with them, they marched. For God had given them concrete symbols of his divine presence: a

26

silver-lined cloud that led them by day and, at night, a pillar bright as fire that lit up the sky.

Then, suddenly, there was chaos. Pharaoh had found out where they were and pursued them. Israel was camped and indeed trapped between high mountains and the swirling sea, and Pharaoh's army was in the gap to their rear. The mountains were too high to climb quickly. Death was there. The sea sang a siren song of impending destruction. Hearing the thunder and seeing the dust of the war chariots, Israel discerned themselves to be hopeless and ensnared. They looked back and forgot about the promises of a glorious future. They looked back, defenseless and alone. They looked back and began to rationalize: "Come to think of it, laboring on the Egyptians' construction jobs wasn't all that bad. Living without joy, peace, and hope could have been worse. Wallowing in anger and confusion for 400 years wasn't completely unbearable. Being down mentally and physically wasn't really all that bad."

Trapped between the mountains and the deep blue sea, Israel continued, "At least we knew what to expect from our enemies. All this talk about a land flowing with milk and honey! You should have left us alone, Moses. We would rather die and be buried in graves in Egypt than drown in the sea. This is your fault, Moses! You made us believe in what we could not see. You made us look to Yahweh. What are you and Yahweh going to do now?"

Like many of us, I remember reading and hearing the Exodus story as a child. It was told as Moses' story. Reading it from that perspective, Moses became my hero. I was in awe of his courage, boldness, leadership, trust, and commitment. Moses was so confident, so strong, and so powerful. And he dominated this story. God would say, "Do this, Moses," and when Moses did what God said, major things began to happen. It was as if all of the events in the story are constructed to allow Moses to become the shining hero.

But lately I have come to wonder whether the significance of this story is about Moses as a hero at all. In addition, what if the point of the passage is *not* about comforting the Hebrews? What if the focus of the story is *not* about the deliverance of Hebrew refugees from drowning? What if this passage is about human doubt, defiance, and desperation in the struggle to be in allegiance with God? What if it is about our looking beyond what we cannot see, about pushing our core faith issues to the surface, about moving beyond seemingly real but ultimately cynical world views and trusting implicitly in God?

The Hebrews were full of anguish, anger, and confusion. They blamed Moses and raised their collective voices against God. Hearing Israel's cries, God addressed their unbelief by simply saying, "Go forward! Do what you were doing before you heard the chariots. Trust me. Keep on moving forward, children of Israel. Forget what was behind and press forward. You have my promises. My assurances are true; I am with you. Remember, I was the one who brought you out of Egypt. Call up the faith that was once within you. Trust me, for I am the Lord thy God.

"Now get up and go forward. Journey on," God urged them. "Journey on when you are discouraged. Journey on when you are desperate. Get up," God said, "and watch me work my glory."

God's response to Israel was simple and straightforward, tailored for a people struggling to find direction, struggling to find one foot to put in front of the other. But to Moses, God's response was characteristic of a relationship. God knew Moses and Moses knew God. So God addressed Moses and said, "But you, you know me intimately. You walk closer to me than most. You discern my direction and follow in my ways. Moses, you carry my vision. You are an encourager for the weaker ones. You are a prayer warrior. Moses! Lift up your staff and stretch out your hand and lead these people forward.

"Lift and stretch," God said. "Lift and stretch out your hand, and receive my Spirit. Lift and stretch, and receive my power. Lift and stretch, and receive my righteousness, my precepts, my direction, my purpose, and my plans for you. Lift your staff, Moses, and stretch out your hand to me. And in so doing, you, through me, will divide the sea and take hold of what your eyes deemed impossible. Take hold of what fear said could not happen. Take hold and know that nothing is too hard for God!"

You know, sometimes when you are between a rock and a deep, wet place, the best thing to do is to keep on doing what you have faithfully done before. This passage was not the first time Moses lifted his staff and stretched his hands upward to God. Can't you see him lifting that staff and stretching his hands and watching the staff become a sanctified serpent consuming Pharaoh's poisonous snakes? Can't you see Moses lifting his staff and stretching his hands and watching water turn to blood, locusts and leaping frogs infest fields, and drought drain the oppressive Egyptian dynasty down to nothing? Moses had experience with lifting his staff and stretching his hands to God. Moses was familiar with receiving from God.

The text says that at the lifting of Moses' hands, God sent the east wind and drove back the sea. That same wind brooded over the face of the deep at Creation, when God lifted his hands and said, "Let there be!" It was the same wind that brought forth a dome in the midst of the waters and separated waters from waters. It was the wind of God, the *Ruach* of God, the Spirit of God, evident from the beginning of creation, that put order in the midst of chaos, freedom in the midst of frenzy. It was that same wind, the very breath of God that breathed and caused us to become living souls. It was the wind, God's breath, God's essence, God's will, that blew as a mighty rushing gale at Pentecost, changing men and women forever. It was the wind of God, the Spirit of God, the complicated yet calming image of God that blew that day. It blows now through us, empowering, shaping, and molding us into the image of God. God sent a manifestation of himself and prepared the way, and Israel walked across on dry land.

God blew, and all that was of God lined up perfectly. God blew, and God's angel moved from a position of guide for the fleeing Hebrews to the position of rear guard to ensure their protection. Likewise, windborne angels protect us. When we lift up the staff and stretch out our hands, those angels push us forward, inhibiting our looking back. They prohibit us from living in the past and succumbing to fears and doubt. The wind-borne angel moved, and so did the cloud and the pillar.

I remember hearing my grandmother, sitting and sewing late at night, singing, "Lord, be a fence all around me everyday. Lord protect me as I travel along this way. I know you can, I know you will. You'll fight my battles if I keep still."

Grandma was calling for wind-borne angels to relocate themselves when she was afraid that past problems might catch up with her. She was calling for clouds and pillars to light her way toward God's tomorrows.

Faith requires that we trust in God. It requires that we hold fast to God's promises when going back appears safer and more attractive. Faith says, "Trust God when all that is in front of you seems to be unending disappointment and strife." Faith says, "Trust and know deep inside that God is God all by himself and faithfulness precedes favor." Know that to trust God is to exalt God, to glorify God, to honor God.

Moses trusted God to soften Pharaoh's heart, and God trusted Moses to lead his people. Moses trusted God to make an expressway in the midst of a raging sea, and God trusted Moses to lift his staff and stretch out his hands.

Do you trust God? Can you say that God trusts you? Can God trust you not to look back, but to put your hand into his and journey forward into the future, depending on his promises? Lift up your staff! Stretch out your hands! You've done it before; do it again. The mountains cannot hinder you. The sea will not circumvent you. Hear the wings of the guardian angels flapping. They will be your front and rear guard, and the seas will open up before you. God will fight your battles and handle your enemies.

Yes, there is a land flowing with milk and honey. God has acted in human history for the purpose of setting you free. It only remains for you to keep on keeping on—to taste the free air and know the unspeakable joy of the love of God, so you wouldn't dare give up or turn around now. Lift up your staff! Stretch out your hands and witness the glorious power of the Lord!

Let Us Prophesy

BY CECELIA WILLIAMS BRYANT

Let us prophesy according to the proportion of faith.
(Romans 12:6)

I am certainly thankful for the stalwart leadership of the Church and for the solidarity of our women. We are here through the suffering love of those sturdy black bridges over which we have crossed.

I was reading an article about the many daughters who were the descendants of Taiwo, and it said something thought-provoking: "We [women], too, are a multitude." When I think about the number of African women, as well as the large number of women from the Diaspora, it is clear to me that "we, too, are a multitude."

Let us pray together to our God that the vision and the power and the life of holiness would be fully manifested throughout African Methodism. Let us further pray that African and diasporic women would seek an open vision. In doing that we will glimpse an alternative ecclesiastical destiny, a new ecclesiology! (And, while we're here, let us pray that we might dismantle the insidious infrastructure of cultural and class domination. I want the brothers to know that when I say "woman" I'm speaking inclusively.)

Beloved, we press toward the fulfillment of our global mandate. It is found in Romans 12:6, in a fragment therein: "Let us prophesy." Let us remember Taiwo. We, too, are a multitude. So we can't keep silent now.

As declared in the book of beginnings, the book of Genesis, from out of a woman came forth the one who would tear Satan's kingdom down! In us the Word of God is made flesh. What we must do in this hour is return to God. Beloved, we have left our first love—but God wants us back! We have mistaken schisms for a source of righteousness—but God wants us back! As African Methodists, we continue to flounder between the illusion of the past and the complexities of the present—yet God still wants us back!

Let us broken women, fierce women—artistic, cultured, and brilliant women—let us prophesy. Wounded women, radical women, this is a call of the Spirit, a call of biblical proportions. This call is intrusive, barging into the matters of our sexuality and our intimacy, micromanaging our relationships. But we remember Deborah, and we know that we can do it! This call is a bit evasive; it does not speak specifically to the economics of being African and being women. There is no program for our social security, but we remember Anna, who was widowed as a young woman but at age eighty-five was found prophesying (see Luke 2:36-38). This call is intense, beloved. It appears to be penetrating from beyond a supernatural reality. This call creates what feels and often looks like emotional instability, or ecclesiastical isolation, or, what is more, relationship purgatory. But we recall Jarena Lee, an unordained A.M.E. preacher in the infant A.M.E. Church, and we know that we can do it.

When we look at the core teachings of the Epistle to the Romans, we discover that God is revealing to the apostle who we really are as the disciples of Jesus Christ. And when we delve into that epistle, we come to know that we are called to be "saints." We're called to be sanctified, set apart, holy as Jesus is holy. We are called to be partakers of the divine nature. As the text reveals to us, we are "justified by faith" (Romans 3:27-28), not by ancestral lineage or good works or gender or knowledge or experience. "Without faith it is impossible to please [God]" (Hebrews 11:6).

She who would prophesy must prophesy according to the *measure* of the faith that she has received. You see, it's faith that makes a real woman! The Syrophenician says that your faith must measure greater than humiliation (see Mark 7:25-29). Mary of Bethany says that your faith must tower over the tenets of propriety and conventional behavior (see Luke 10:40-42). Bishop Vashti McKenzie teaches us that our faith must be more profound and run deeper than ecclesiastical politics. Without just such a measure of faith, it is not possible to prophesy!

Paul refers to prophecy as the "best gift." He says, "I would that you all would prophesy" (see 1 Corinthians 14:5). And what's exciting to me is this: Paul says that if you want the gift of prophecy, "*Pray* for it." Jeremiah says you know when you've got it: It's like fire, shut up in your bones (see Jeremiah 20:9).

My sisters, God has prepared us in this hour for promotion. But let us not be deceived as some have been. Sampson says, "Beware of whose lap you put your head in" (see Judges 16:18-19). Jonah says to beware of the direction you're taking when you hear from God. Job says, "Beware of becoming unequally yoked" (see Job 2:9-10). Whoever, whatever I give the power to separate me from holiness, that is the power to whom I surrender my prophetic light, until the light in me becomes darkness (see Romans 1:28-32) and I am no longer the woman that Jesus died for me to be. Paul realistically records that when people followed a lie, the lie began to shape who they were; and worst of all, they began to take pleasure in those who resisted the spirit of the Lord.

My sisters, we can no longer stagger under the weight of our unbelief. Let us pray to God to strengthen our faith. My sisters, we, too, are a multitude. As we wrestle with the implications of our predicament, cite says this: "Our goal is not to become powerful—but to become holy. God promises to empower that which God *first* makes holy. If we are becoming the people God calls his own, we must listen to God. As our trust in God increases, we should be growing in holiness." A mature Christian will be both holy *and* powerful. But holiness precedes power.

This is the hour that God has chosen women to be a manifestation of his glory, so let us prophesy! The forces of the anti-Christ are many and powerful. And not all who prophesy will be justly recognized, ordained, or elected—or receive an appointment! Nevertheless, we, too, are a multitude, so let us prophesy! We were born for this.

Africa's daughters have been anointed to prophesy and to heal: Mai Chaza of Zimbabwe; Alice Lenshina Mulenga of Zambia; Marie Lalou of the Ivory Coast; Etta Sherman of Liberia; Dorothy Morris of Guyana, the first woman presiding elder of African Methodism; Sarah Francis Davis of Texas; Carolyn Guidry of California—we were born for this! So let us prophesy. We were called to this. Called out of obscurity, called out of supposed insanity, called out of poverty, called out of ignorance, called out of shame. Yes, called out of vanity, called out of "success."

God accepts only one answer. Do you know what that answer is? *Yes!* "For the gifts and calling of God are without repentance" (Romans 11:29). So let us prophesy! Like women who have slept with the enemy, but who like Hagar woke up in the wilderness and found the well of the God who hears and answers prayer (see Genesis 16:6-14), let us prophesy!

Let's prophesy like it's a Friday morning and the men are hiding and we are anticipating great obstacles, but we'll get where we're going. We won't find what we're looking for, but we'll get what we need. Let us prophesy as though Pentecost has come (see Acts 2:17) and we are the ones that Joel had in mind (see Joel 2:28).

Watchman Nee says you can prophesy if the presence of God is in your life. Frangipani says you can prophesy if you are holy. Paul says you can prophesy if you have a measure of faith. Jesus says, "You can prophesy if you abide in me and my word abides in you."

So let us prophesy an invisible kingdom to a technological world. So let us prophesy the gospel of new life to a culture where death is entertainment and violence is erotic. So let us prophesy holiness to a generation whose mantra is "keeping it real." Let us prophesy: Holiness, until justice rolls down like waters and righteousness like a mighty stream (see Amos 5:24). Let us prophesy: Holiness, until comes a new heaven and a new earth. Let us prophesy: Holiness, until the church militant becomes the church triumphant!

Prophesy! Prophesy! Prophesy!

Dance with My Father

BY RENITA J. WEEMS

When she got off her donkey, Caleb asked her,
"What can I do for you?" She replied, "Do me a special favor.
Since you have given me land in the Negev, give me also springs of
water." So Caleb gave her the upper and lower springs.
(Joshua 15:18-19, NIV)

"Tell me about your father." It's the kind of request with voltage enough to reduce grown, intelligent, successful women to wailing, snotty-nosed, stammering girls. Coming to grips with the possibility that your childhood experiences with your father are even now influencing your reality is a shocking revelation to most women. Bring up the topic of my father and I withdraw from the conversation.

We spend much of our adult lives blaming our mothers for what they didn't give us, or for giving us too much of the wrong thing, but it's different with our fathers. We hardly knew what to expect of the men who passed in and out of our lives. Therapists are beginning to help us understand that what a father gives—or fails to give—his daughter affects her experiences with other men, affects her experiences of love, family, career, and, above all, her image of God *the Father*.

For Caleb's daughter Achsah, the desert princess, the time came when she would have to figure out how to get past blaming her father for her plight as a daughter and a woman and discover how to find water in the desert. In Joshua 15 you will find that Achsah went overnight from being the daughter of a celebrated clan leader named Caleb to becoming the wife of a renowned man named Othniel, who was destined to become one of the leading judges in Israel. She had learned much in her father's house about living in a man's world—she was the only daughter among four brothers (see 1 Chronicles 2:48-49)—which had made her, no doubt, the apple of her daddy's eye.

The writer of the book of Numbers immortalizes Caleb as an uncommonly positive man. After spying out the land with Joshua, Caleb spoke with confidence and enthusiasm about the people of God being able to take the Promised Land, despite the presence of giants. What he thought about raising a daughter we can only guess, but we do know that at age eighty-five, Caleb took seriously his obligation as a father to find the most suitable son-in-law for his daughter. He would arrange a marriage for his daughter that would form alliances, expand territories, and secure the family's future.

Centuries ago, daughters had no choice in such matters. A woman's identity was embedded in her role as daughter, wife, sister, niece, or whatever. Female children learned early that their status and circumstances were bound to their ability to please the men in their family. There is no evidence that Achsah protested her father's decision. But that doesn't mean she didn't have any feelings about what was happening in her life. A part of her probably secretly hoped that Caleb would change his mind about marrying her off to Othniel. Deep down Achsah probably felt betrayed by her father. But Caleb was a product of his culture.

We know only too well the stories in the Bible about fathers and daughters that confirm this authoritarian image of fathers. Because a daughter was a father's property, his honor was tied to his ability to safeguard her chastity. Whole chapters are given to stories about a father avenging the rape of his daughter (Jacob and Dinah, Genesis 34), a father sacrificing his daughter's virginity and life to keep his vow to God (Jepthah and his daughter, Judges 11), a father switching daughters in order to extend his son-in-law's service to him (Laban, Rachel, and Leah, Genesis 29), and a father too inebriated to care about or notice his sexual advances toward his daughters (Lot and his daughters, Genesis 19).

If our relationships as fathers and daughters were limited to the script bequeathed us in these stories, a daughter would be wise to fear and loathe the man she calls "Father." But that is not the case. There are other father-daughter stories in the Bible (e.g., Jairus and his daughter,

Mark 5 or Luke 8; or Phillip and his four daughters, Acts 21:8-9)—positive ones that can heal daughters who were wounded by fathers who turned them into objects and that can heal fathers wounded by the effects of patriarchy.

The story of Caleb and Achsah rises above the tragic. Achsah figured out a way to tap into the side of her that was good and most like her father—her enthusiasm, her quick thinking, her ability to plan and to set a plan in motion, her gift of persuasion—and made all of these attributes work for her purposes.

The narrator insists that Othniel, Achsah's husband, was the one to urge his wife to press her father for a more lucrative dowry. That's probably because the thought of a woman, even a cherished only daughter, approaching her father with such a bold request was hard for our narrator to imagine. But I don't doubt for a moment that Achsah had settled in her mind already that she needed more from her father than the dry, arid desert of the Negev which he'd apportioned for her dowry (see Joshua 15:19). Achsah had heard Caleb recount the story of God's people's beginning as wandering nomads, their sojourn into Egyptian slavery, and their glorious deliverance out of slavery by God's outstretched hand. She was aware that the land represented their future. She knew as much about these things as Othniel. Fertile land especially—as "land flowing with milk and honey"—was the desire of every desert princess and prince. Achsah needed a chance to secure her future. She had no choice but to acquiesce to her father's choice for her husband, but she refused to play the role of hapless victim.

She dismounted her donkey when she saw her father. She'd rehearsed how best to phrase her request. But standing in front of her father that day for the first time since her marriage to Othniel, not daddy's little girl any more, but a woman, the most charming way to approach her father vanished. The words just blurted out of Achsah's mouth: "Grant me a blessing, Father!" Then she added, "You have given me the Negev, now give me also springs of water" (author's paraphrase). Achsah needed tillable, irrigated property as part of her dowry. This would secure her place in her husband's household. Even though the land a wife brought to her marriage became the property of her husband, the fact is that by law a husband could never dispose of the property without suffering substantial loss himself.

Caleb granted his daughter her request without hesitation. Here, Jesus' words to his disciples come to mind: "If you then, though you are evil, know how to give good gifts to your children, how much more will your Father in heaven give the Holy Spirit to those who ask him!" (Luke 11:13, NIV). Instead of despising her father for what his culture wouldn't allow him to give his daughter, Achsah found a way to accept from her father what he could give. He gave her an inheritance, land.

Some inheritances come in the form of memories. As I peered down at my father as he lay in a coma in the hospital last year, listening to the hard, raspy sounds of his erratic breathing, staring at his filmy eyes, watching his body involuntarily twitching as he began the long, hard journey of disentangling himself from this life and struggling to focus on the light that would guide him into the next life (what the old folks called "traveling"), I knew the time had come for me to let go of him—the father I knew and the father I would never know. There was no more energy left in either of us to hold up our end of the fight. I sat at his bedside as he traveled mindlessly; I turned the pages of the Bible and read because I thought that was what I should do as a minister of the gospel. My heart wasn't in it, not really, but I read on. It was either that or listen to the sounds of him wrenching himself from this present age.

"Though my father and mother forsake me, the LORD will receive me," I heard myself reading (Psalm 27:10, NIV). I stopped. I couldn't recall that verse being a part of Psalm 27. The psalm was a favorite of mine, but I only knew it as far as the fifth verse: "For he will hide me in his shelter in the day of trouble; he will conceal me under the cover of his tent; he will set me high on a rock" (NRSV). I paused to see if there was any change in my father's breathing. No change. *Just like you, Pop,* I thought. *Pretending not to hear what you don't want to hear.* I read on.

That night as my father lay dying in his hospital bed and I sat trying to comfort him (and myself) by reading random passages from the Bible, a strange thing happened. The nurse had turned the television around to face my father's side of the room for no apparent reason, except that God had used her to do it. God intervened that night through the lyrics of a song playing softly on the television. Above the din of my mumbling Scripture, the sound of Luther Vandross's hauntingly beautiful song to his own father, "Dance with my Father," seeped into the hospital room. The song soulfully recalls memories of Luther's father dancing with his mother, of his father frolicking with him, carrying him to bed, and Luther pleads with God to let his father return for one last encore with him—or better yet, with his mother. It was enough to break the heart. The tears wouldn't stop coming. Not from my father, but from me. Suddenly the odor in the county hospital room changed. The smell of my father's decaying flesh gave way to what I can only describe now as the smell of fresh rain. That's it. Rain. It was the smell of an afternoon rain after a long, dry spell, a rain that leaves the earth yearning for more but content to lap up what it can get.

The story of Achsah and Caleb teaches us that a father's daughter reconciles with the memory and life of her father only when she can come to grips with his true gifts. His true gifts are the ones he actually was capable of giving and generously lavished on her: his sense of humor, his love for learning, his discipline, his candor, his forgiving spirit, or his love for music. For me, it was the memory of my father picking me up from the floor, where as a girl I'd fallen asleep watching wrestling matches on television, and carrying me in his arms up to bed and tucking me in. These gifts are only apparent and available when a daughter dismounts her donkey and is ready to claim what is hers, to release feeling hurt about those things her father was never able to give her.

The only hope a daddy's girl has for drying her tears, growing up, and living beyond the wounds her father inflicted upon her is to accept her father for the man he was and release him from the man she fantasized him being but never was.

But Grow in Grace

BY LOIS B. FORTSON

But grow in grace, and in the knowledge of our
Lord and Saviour Jesus Christ.
(2 Peter 3:18)

I t's the year's end, and it is at this time that lots of people traditionally make vows for the ensuing year. Young women vow to lose weight. Young men vow to work out regularly at the gym. As we mature, we vow to give up smoking, drinking, gambling, profanity, gossiping—you name it. The only trouble is that we almost always fail to keep these vows, no matter how good our original intentions.

One reason for our failure is that the vows are negative. We vow to *stop* doing something, or to give up something. When we attempt to discard a bad habit, it leaves a dangerous vacuum. The nervous smoker needs something to do with his hands. The fattening foods taste much better than the healthy foods that are supposed to fill the void. The late sleep we give up is far more enjoyable than the sweating at a gym that takes its place. So we don't do what we said we would, and it leaves a tempting hole in our consciousness.

Another reason the vows fail is implied in Ecclesiastes 12, where we are taught to remember our Creator in the days of our youth, before our bad habits are squelched by old age (see 12:1). In other words, we need to set our good habits while we're young and pliable. The older we get, the harder it is to change our living patterns. If we have gorged ourselves and stretched our stomachs for decades, we are less and less willing and able to follow a healthy diet.

The difficulty increases as we look at our spiritual habits. Our text makes me realize that I don't recall ever actually making any such vows in the spiritual realm. And I don't recall any of my friends mentioning such a New Year's pledge, either. Let's try this on for a New Year's vow: Grow in grace. If we are young, it may be easier because our hearts are not yet hardened, as mentioned in Ecclesiastes. But at every age, every one of us is urgently called to grow next year "in grace and in the knowledge of our Lord and Saviour Jesus Christ" (2 Peter 3:18).

What on earth is this grace, and how do we grow in it? Well, first of all, it's the capacity to forgive people. We vow to grow in our ability to give unmerited acceptance and empathetic understanding to people who treat us unjustly, which is the way God treats us. The opposite action is to hold our anger and hostility, which is worse for our health than even cholesterol and alcohol. Obviously, it makes sense to vow to grow in grace, if just for our health.

But grace goes further; it takes the initiative to be generous and helpful to all, especially to those in great need. Jesus himself affirmed his calling to help the needy when he stood to read from Isaiah (see Luke 4:18-19). In a later parable, Jesus flatly declared that when we are gracious to the hungry and homeless, we are gracious to God (see Matthew 25:40). To grow in grace is to grow in thoughtful generosity.

A third definition, which I suppose is the most common definition of grace, is that quality of personality that stays, as we say, "cool" in tense situations. A recent issue of *Sports Illustrated* rightfully praises Dave Robinson and Tim Duncan as Sportsmen of the Year (December 15, 2003), but the chief aspect of it all is their calm graciousness under fire. They have grown in grace.

The question at this point, of course, is, "How do *we* manage to grow in grace?" The author of the words of our text is Peter, an ex-fisherman, and the story of his growth in grace may very well help to answer this question. The record affirms that Peter was a cursing loud-mouth, used to aggressively saying whatever he wanted to say. He started on the rough side, but he didn't stay there. We can figure out what Peter means in this text when we look and see how he himself grew in grace.

Peter was a tough sailor and the boss of a boat crew. He had strong muscles and a commanding presence. He had a fishing business and a great knowledge of fish—their habits and their behavior. He knew when to let down his casting net and how the net fell as the weights dragged it down. (The net took the shape of a dome and enclosed the fish.) Peter was very self-confident, if not downright arrogant.

But then he worked one whole night and didn't catch anything. He was tired, his crew was tired, and he was ready to call it a night. But something happened just about when he was ready to give up. Jesus entered into Peter's boat and said, "Launch out into the deep, and after you have launched out, let down your net" (Luke 5:4, author's paraphrase). Peter replied, "Jesus, Master, we have toiled all night long, and we have caught absolutely nothing. Nevertheless, if you say so, Jesus, I will humor you. I'll go along, Jesus. I'll do what you say, but I don't believe anything is going to happen. I'll go through the motions of serving you, but I don't really believe that things are going to change for me. You see, I know about this fishing business" (see 5:5).

Peter then did as Jesus had commanded, and suddenly he had so many fish in the dome of his net that it began to break open. They had to call other crews to come and help. When Peter saw all this, he fell at Jesus' knees and, looking at himself, he realized how sinful he was. He said to Jesus, "Depart from me, Jesus. I'm just a loud talkin', cussin' sailor. I'm no good, Jesus" (see 5:8). Lesson one: Humility is the beginning of grace.

The second lesson in growing in grace is this: Stay close to Jesus. The Lord knows how to make things happen, and all of us can be helped to be more humble and gracious if in our minds we are trying and if our hearts are open to the gracious action of the Holy Spirit. This fishing scene was early in the morning, and it was before the break of dawn when Peter and the others drew nigh to the shore. They could see a figure of a man; it was Jesus waiting for them, standing by the Sea of Galilee. I don't know how Jesus comes, but he comes when we need him the most. Jesus will come to the place where you work—when you least expect it. When you are tired, worn, and discouraged, feeling bad about yourself, he comes and provides the trust that gives you calm. It's good to have a habit of hanging out with Jesus. Grace doesn't grow in isolation and fatigue.

Not only will Jesus come on your job; he will get into your business. Jesus knew exactly who Peter was and all about his past, but Jesus was concerned about Peter's future. Jesus said, "Just follow me. Connect with me, Peter; I'm going someplace. Follow me." This invitation offers a reason for being and a life abundant with the satisfaction of leadership and service. Jesus said, "Just follow me, and I'm going to teach you how to draw people. Stick with me, Peter" (see 5:10). And Peter became the instant leader of the disciples—the spokesman. The crowds obeyed him, and he enjoyed telling 5,000 people where to sit. Even Jesus' disciples looked to him to speak first. Peter was growing in the many phases of grace. But he let this popularity be his downfall.

Peter missed a step. He was in the habit of taking over the leadership of crowds, but he slipped up. He enjoyed it too much, and for the wrong, egotistic reason, rather than for the joy of service, of doing the will of his Lord. Jesus had warned the disciples of his crucifixion and of the pressures they would face. He had said they would desert him, but Peter had spoken up quickly and said, "Aw, no! *I* would never deny you, Lord. I would *die* for you, Lord." Jesus looked at him and prophesied, "This very night, before the cock crows, you will deny me three times" (see Matthew 26:33-34; Mark 14:29-30; Luke 22:33-34; John 13:37-38). And that's exactly what Peter did; his ego won out over his trust and gracious faithfulness.

After Jesus was arrested, a bystander identified Peter as one of the twelve, and Peter lied. Nobody believed him, and he tried to take over a second time. Panic arose in Peter, and when he denied Jesus the third time, he tried to strengthen it with a few choice words of his old profanity. As he denied Jesus this third time, he looked up and realized that Jesus had heard him. The look on Jesus' face nearly broke Peter's heart. The rooster crowed, and Peter went out and wept bitterly. That's when he *really* grew in grace, because he had repented.

Peter's next big test was on the day of Pentecost, when the disciples were gathered and everyone was filled with the Holy Spirit. The unbelievers in the crowd started mocking Peter and his audience, accusing them of being drunk, but Peter replied by preaching with great power: "These men are not drunk, as you suppose. . . . This is what was spoken by the prophet Joel: 'In the last days, God says, I will pour out my Spirit . . . upon all people. Your sons and your daughters will prophesy, your young men shall see visions, your old men dream dreams'" (Acts 2:15-17, NIV). It must have been a great sermon, full of grace, for thousands accepted Christ that day.

Peter had grown in grace. He wasn't afraid anymore. He was filled with the Holy Spirit. A little later on, he stood in court and testified of the beggar he had healed: "This man was healed in the name and power of Jesus Christ . . . the man whom you crucified" (Acts 4:10, author's paraphrase). Even though this court could have sentenced Peter to death, Peter went right on preaching: "This same Jesus who you rejected has become the chief cornerstone of many a life. There is salvation in no other name" (4:11-12, author's paraphrase). Peter had grown a lot. He had come a long, long way from where he started.

I am praying this New Year for all of us to grow in grace and in the knowledge of our Lord. I want to grow where Peter grew to. "I want to be like Jesus in my heart, Lord; I want to be a Christian in my heart."

Tabitha, Arise;
Dorcas, Get Up!

BY CASSANDRA A. SPARROW

This woman was full of good works and almsdeeds
which she did. . . . Peter put them all forth, and kneeled down,
and prayed; and turning him to the body said, Tabitha, arise.
And she opened her eyes: and when she saw Peter, she sat up.
(Acts 9:36,40)

Today we want to look more closely at the life of one of the disciples of Christ who lived in the city called Joppa, a Mediterranian seaport some thirty-five miles northwest of Jerusalem. Dorcas, called Tabitha in Aramaic, was an affluent woman who supplied the cloth she made into clothing for the poor. Among the widows of the sailors lost at sea, and especially among the poor children, she was noted for providing colorful garments.

Yes, she was a vessel of honor, for whom many people were thankful to God. The townspeople were particularly aware that Tabitha could have just rested in her home on the hill. She could have just relaxed as she watched the needy pass to and fro along the waterfront. Yet she not only bought and donated cloth; she also sewed garments out of it with her own hands. Luke, author of the book of Acts, says this of her: "Now there was at Joppa a certain disciple named Tabitha, which by interpretation is called Dorcas: this woman was full of good works and almsdeeds which she did" (Acts 9:36). Her reputation for helping people was widely known.

This testimony represents a snapshot of what could be a model for all of us. Tabitha's gracious helpfulness was like a light on a hill. She was always to be seen wherever there was need throughout the community, always willing to lend a helping hand. When someone died she was there, cooking something for the family, doing whatever she could to help. If she learned about that last rain storm, or a hurricane, or a flood, she would be the one to provide dry blankets, shawls, food and water, and other items. She tried to see that people were cared for in any circumstance.

Tabitha was a dedicated Christian. She was indeed a jewel in the kingdom—of far more value than rubies. She expressed genuine love to all who were blessed by her caring ministry. If around today, perhaps Tabitha would be the one to assist the many busy mothers. She would make sure they had enough food to lunch on, that they had a way to get to work, that cars were fueled up, or that they had access to a car pool. She would have been good about finding dependable child care. She might also have helped to feed and find clothing for the people we call homeless. She was *"full* of good works" (emphasis added).

Do you know someone like Tabitha? When I think of people like Tabitha, I think of the saying that goes something like this:
>   1. There are some people who are wishbones, always hoping
>   someone else would do it;
>   2. There are some people who are jawbones—all talk, no action;
>   3. And then there are the backbones, those folk who get the job
>   done, who are there through thick and thin.

Do you know what I mean? Well, what happens when these "backbone" folk are not around?

"And it came to pass in those days, that she [Tabitha] was sick, and died: whom when they had washed, they laid her in an upper chamber" (9:37). Yes, Tabitha got sick. We don't know what caused her to become sick. If Joppa was somewhere like Washington, D.C., Baltimore, Richmond, or any other city today, when she got sick we would have suspected cancer, diabetes, heart trouble, and the list goes on. Who knows what could have made her sick? Perhaps she was, like some of the Tabithas of today, stretched too thin, overloaded, trying to do her work and everybody else's at the same time. Maybe she just gave and gave until she wore herself out. Whatever it was, we won't continue to hazard a diagnosis. All we know is what the text says: She got sick. In fact, the text goes further and says she got sick and died. They washed her to make her ready for burial, and they laid her out in an upper chamber.

Tabitha's sisters and brothers in Christ were drifting in their minds between "Oh, how unselfish and giving she was" and "What shall we do now?" We can relate anew to how they felt at Joppa. Paul himself said something of the same sort in Philippians 1:3-5: "I thank my God upon every remembrance of you, always in every prayer of mine for you all making request with joy, for your fellowship in the gospel from the first day until now." But neither we nor they could stop with tears and pleasant memories. They had to do something more than that, for this was such a great loss to the church and the community. "Tabitha, Tabitha, we love you and we will miss you, but we had better send for Pastor Peter right away."

Luke continues his account: "And forasmuch as Lydda was nigh to Joppa, and the disciples had heard that Peter was there, they sent unto him two men, desiring him that he would not delay to come to them" (9:38). It wasn't that the people were expecting a miracle; perhaps they just wanted some guidance as to how to deal with their grief and how to fill in for the loss to the church and its ministries. They just wanted to hear a word from the Lord. "Hurry up, Peter! Somebody help! Call the doctors, call the elders of the church. Can't somebody please help us? Isn't there anything to be done for poor Tabitha? She did so much for others."

Luke records Peter's answer to their plea in verse thirty-nine: "Then Peter arose and went with them [the two men who were sent]. When he was come, they brought him into the upper chamber: and all the widows stood by him weeping, and showing the coats and garments which Dorcas made, while she was with them." They were weeping, trying to share the load of grief which weighed so heavily upon them all. They were interceding and pouring out their prayers. They were trying to calm themselves with words of praise for Tabitha: "Look at all these dresses and coats and robes and sandals that Tabitha sewed. Aren't they just lovely!" With all this talking, the people knew that they needed help.

They had sounded the alarm, sent for help, and now Peter had come.

He had seen them in their misery, and it didn't take him long to act. As Luke records it, "[He] put them all forth, and kneeled down, and prayed; and turning him to the body said, Tabitha, arise. And she opened her eyes: and when she saw Peter, she sat up" (Acts 9:40). Through the power of our risen Savior, one of Christ's disciples, Peter, was at the bedside raising Tabitha from the dead. Jesus said in the great commission in Mark 16:18, "They shall lay hands on the sick and they shall recover." And so it was fulfilled.

Luke's record concludes, "And he gave her his hand, and lifted her up, and when he had called the saints and widows, presented her alive. And it was known throughout all Joppa; and many believed in the Lord" (9:41-42). Their joy was unspeakable, and the number of converts was awesome.

But what does all this mean for us? We were not witnesses to the risen Dorcas, nor can we say in detail exactly what happened. We certainly haven't seen any resurrections recently. But we here have all seen the living spirit of Dorcas herself, as she is still expressed in service. We can witness to the fact that all over Christendom there are Dorcas Circles and other women's groups bearing her name. They are carrying on and extending the ministry that Dorcas modeled. There is no greater memorial to her, or to anyone, than this. Christian women all over the world are eager to earn the level of sincere praise heaped on Tabitha when it was too late for her to hear it. There can be no more fitting memorial to Dorcas or to our ancestors or to ourselves than that it be said of us that we used all our skills and poured out all we had from ploughs to sewing machines to the latest computers to meet the needs of this present age.

In places all over the globe, it's time once again for Tabitha to come to life. Those who are asleep or nearing the throes of institutional death need to awaken and arise like Tabitha. And the young and discouraged and old and tired need to claim the unspeakable joy of waking up and "getting up" in the service of our Lord.

The greatest joy of all came after the word of Tabitha's resurrection had spread. Luke wrote, "Many believed in the Lord" (9:42). The revitalization of Tabitha meant more souls were saved, brought to Christ. A revival broke out. People heard of and believed in Jesus' power.

Today, the joy of serving Jesus and living the abundant life is still without equal. Ministers and laity have the privilege of spreading the Word and witness of God in every community. It's time to use the skills we have as Tabitha did with her sewing. It doesn't have to be a great public ministry, but it may be something that we do in the quietness of our homes. It may be the daily phone calls to seniors, or taking them to get groceries, or mobilizing them to vote for peace and justice. It may be that visit of encouragement. Do what your hands find to do this very day, for AIDS vicitims, addicts, alcoholics, and abused folk who must be healed.

Tabithas of today, arise! Dorcases of this decade, get up, so that others may see your good works and glorify your Father in heaven, so that your testimony shed abroad may bring others to Christ, even as did Dorcas at Joppa. Tabithas, get up, so that you can resume your places of worship in the sanctuary and service in the streets and with those in need. Tabithas, get up, and preach the gospel. Sing like you ought; usher the sheep into the sanctuary. Tabitha, Tabitha, the Lord is speaking to you. Tabitha, arise; Dorcas, get up!

The Main Issue

BY J. RUTH TRAVIS

One thing I know, that, whereas I was blind, now I see.
(John 9:25)

Whatever the circumstance, wherever you are, whatever your condition, you can be assured that Jesus sees you and can help you. In Jesus' day, the only thing a blind man could do was to beg, and that was exactly what the man in our story was doing when Jesus passed by. There may have been other people present who needed to be healed, but Jesus saw and selected this man. The disciples saw him too, but not really as a man who needed healing, not as an object of mercy. They wanted to engage in a theological discussion with Jesus: "Rabbi, who sinned, this man or his parents, that he was born blind?" (John 9:2, NIV). Jesus answered, "Neither this man nor his parents sinned . . . but this happened so that the work of God might be displayed in his life. As long as it is day, we must do the work of him who sent me. Night is coming, when no one can work" (9:3-5, NIV).

This is where the disciples made a big mistake. It was none of their business why the man was born blind. Their role as associates of Jesus did not call for them to label this blind man before they examined his total condition. They should have looked before they labeled, if indeed they were called to label at all. This man was a beggar and in need of help right now! They were not thinking about how this man had spent his whole life in a world of darkness. They never considered the fact that the man could hear them talking about him. They seemed too happy talking about his sin. They wanted to discuss all that might be wrong in the man's life.

We repeat this same mistake every time we also fail to look before we label. It is good to put a label on a jelly jar or a manila folder so we can tell what is on the inside. But we also put labels on people, assuming that we can judge them as quickly or as accurately as if they were a jar of jelly. We forget that Jesus warned us not to judge, lest we be judged the same way (see Matthew 7:1). We are heard saying things like, "He doesn't look at all like he has any character," "What does a fine young man like him see in her?" or "What on earth do they see in that preacher?"

The disciples likewise applied a label. They missed the main issue. They looked past the fact that the man was a lifelong beggar and in desperate need of help. They were utterly insensitive to the fact that the man could hear their merciless banter about him. All they wanted was an intriguing theological discussion about the possible results of sin. They no doubt assumed that there had to be some juicy discussion material hidden in the poor fellow's biography.

Risking being guilty of this very kind of sin, I am drawn to wonder what on earth could make these close followers of Jesus be so insensitive. The first thing that comes to mind is the fact that it is much easier to talk about a needy person than it is to roll up your sleeves and help that person. It is easier to debate homosexuality than it is to befriend a falsely accused gay person. It is easier to discuss divorce than it is to help a person who has just had to endure the trauma of a family break-up. It is easier to oppose abortion than it is to support an orphanage that houses the lives that were saved by saving every fetus. It is easier to complain about problems in the welfare system than it is to provide supplementary assistance in instances of crying need. The real issue is not about what I think. It is about what I did to help. Unfortunately, it is easier to label than to love.

So, as we return to the story of the blind man, we find Jesus *doing* something that changed the man's situation. His comments in response to the disciples' doctrinal inquiry were very brief. The details of what he did were a bit earthy, but Jesus' compound of spit and mud, spread over the man's eyes, changed the man's situation. Then he gave the man a part in his own healing and sent him to "go, wash in the Pool of Siloam" (9:7). The man went where he was told to go, did what he was told to do, and came back seeing a world he had never seen before.

Jesus didn't label the man; he helped him. He was more concerned about the man's future than about his past. The main issue wasn't about the sightless man's background, nor about that of his parents. Where people came from isn't important to God, nor are how many mistakes they made while there. Our backgrounds may be full of barstools, back-alley arrangements, wrong relationships with the wrong people, and rebellion against the very will of God. But God is not, as we say, "bent out of shape" over where we came from or what we came out of. God's main concern is where we are *going*.

As Jesus was concerned with where the blind man could go from there, so also is God's concern for us about where we will go, and so ought to be our concern as well. We need to know that the bottom line in the life of any human being is in God's hands. After we have done what we can to help, that person is God's concern, not ours. The situation is in God's much safer hands, since God sees and knows all about the folk we were called to help and all about us who are trying to obey and help. The risk of assigning us the job of labeling God's children was far too great for him to take. Think how cruel and inaccurate our labels might have turned out to be!

Now, finally, notice how the healed man himself defined the main issue for the crowd as well as for the busybody, theologically nosy disciples. The neighbors pressed him, and he stuck to the main issue: "Jesus took spit, made mud, and put it on my face. He told me to wash it off in the pool of Siloam, and I walked away seeing. What else is there to say?"

The neighbors were not satisfied with this, so they took the formerly blind man to the Pharisees (church officials), who put him through the same grueling questions. Like the disciples, the Pharisees confused the issue with doctrinal discussion about the proper way to observe the Sabbath. Again the healed man calmly held his ground and stuck to the main issue. The Pharisees, unwilling to give up, turned to the man's parents to ask if what the man said was really true. Afraid that a true answer would get them in trouble, they took the Fifth Amendment, so to speak, and referred the inquisitors back to their son. "He's grown up. Let him speak for himself." So for the fourth time, the previously blind man went to the heart of the matter, the main issue. He made it brief. In the common language of his day, he said, "I haven't a clue as to where Jesus is, and I don't know anything about all those questions about him being a sinner. I just know one thing, that though I was blind, now I see. Period."

The main issue is still the same in the Church of Jesus Christ as it was in this story. There is a need for churches to engage in theological discussion, to check against errors, some of which can be quite dangerous. Call it meddling into God's business, at times like these in our story, or call it theological self-examination in healthier endeavors. But, when people are in dire need of whatever kind, even a sincere, on-the-spot review of doctrinal principles is out of order.

It's time to do what Jesus quite obviously would have done were he here. Churches of today need to return to being a fellowship of souls whose word to the world is like the blind man's: "Whereas I once was blind, now I see; whereas I once had migraine headaches, now I'm free of pain; whereas I once had a terrible temper, now I'm calm and understanding and peaceful; whereas I once was lost to a crack habit, now I'm clean of all drugs and happy in the Lord, like I have never been happy before; whereas I once was crushed under the load of HIV, a church of the Lord Jesus Christ found medical care and medicine for me, and the prickly threads of my once hopeless life are lengthened out, and my gracious God has bid my golden moments to roll on."

The main goal of the Church of Jesus Christ is the saving of souls, but Jesus made a much wider definition of saving ministry than many of us have today. Jesus read his definition at the church at Nazareth, where he grew up: "The Spirit of the Lord is upon me, for he has anointed me" (Luke 14:18). He was to preach the gospel to the poor, and the common people heard him gladly. He was to heal the brokenhearted, and he promised, "I will not leave you comfortless" (see John 14:18). He was to proclaim liberty to the captives, for we shall know the truth, and it shall set us free (see John 8:32). He was to proclaim recovery of sight to the blind, and in Matthew Jesus said, "The blind receive their sight" (11:5). He was to set at liberty those who are oppressed, and Peter's first sermon reported that Jesus went about doing good and healing all who were oppressed of the devil (see Acts 10:38). He was to proclaim the acceptable year of the Lord (see Luke 4:19).

Paul said that the Spirit of God told him that now is the acceptable time; "now is the day of salvation" (2 Corinthians 6:2). The personal testimony of the blind man Jesus healed is the most powerful word possible, and we strive for the day when thousands in every city and county, every state and country, every region and remnant of Mother Earth, will be testifying for the world to hear:

> We know very little about the intricacies of theology,
> Or the traditions of the established churches.
> But this one, unforgettable experience is ours to treasure,
> That Jesus opened our eyes and gave us sight.

A Word for the Weary

BY MARY H. YOUNG

And ye shall seek me, and find me,
when ye shall search for me with all your heart.
(Jeremiah 29:13)

Couched in the context of the first Jewish deportation to Babylon, the word in this text is for both Israel and for us. God had declared that the time would come when "exile" for Israel would not be a choice, but rather an "existential reality." No longer would they be at ease in Jerusalem, but according to God's plan, they would pay for their unfaithfulness. As the prophets before Jeremiah had already prophesied, Israel did indeed go into near-slavery. And now, having been in captivity for only a short while, they were weary, confused, and bewildered. Their unrest had been fueled by prophets and priests of both the homeland Jerusalem and those in the Diaspora who had declared that God was going to break the yoke of King Nebuchadnezzar and send the children back home. On the lips of Jeremiah, however, was a different word for those whose lot for the time being was to live in a strange land.

It is a word assuring us that God is a just God, and that if a person really wants to be close to God, he or she must also suffer the consequences of infidelity to God. We can't treat God any old way and expect to slide by unscathed! It is a word that affirms our destiny to wait on God—the one who knows the plans made for us. Israel's period of waiting in a grim and threatening world of exile could not be rushed. There would be years of spiritual discipline necessary to lead them toward repentance and peace with God.

Could it be that every now and then you and I also need this unique opportunity for a "Babylonian experience" in which God coddles us in a crucible of correction, takes us to the potter's house and works a work on us with the potter's wheel, breaks us and makes us into new vessels? This word for the weary comes with two aspects of its own power and validity. Jeremiah offers a word that has both purpose and promise.

The *purpose* of this captivity was clear. For years Israel had sought her own; her priests and prophets had gone astray; the hearts of the children had been turned from the fathers. The proverbial saying that "the fathers had eaten bitter grapes, setting the children's teeth on edge" had become a reality. God would not deliver Israel from that which she needed to experience. Some time in captivity was a given. The southern kingdom (Judah) would be under Babylon for a while. Though the voice of self-made prophets would try to circumvent God's plan, suffering was a necessity. It was God's doing that now, at last, Israel would come face-to-face with her own estrangement from him. Little did Israel know that no matter how others tried to define what God was doing, God's plan for her was wrapped up in *Kairos* time, which could not be merely counted or measured by chronological exactness, but rather by Israel's willingness to seek God with her whole heart.

Jeremiah's word of purpose was: Forget what Zedekiah, Hananiah, and the others have said about checking out early. You are going to be in Babylon for a while. Don't let them fill your heads with dreams of a speedy return to Jerusalem. They are not sent from the Lord, but are instruments of their own imaginations. Go ahead, build some houses and settle down. Plant gardens from which to eat and feed your families. Make sure that your sons and daughters are marrying and bearing children, so that your heritage might remain. Seek the peace and prosperity of the city to which you have gone. Pray for it, because if you want your own deliverance you've got to concentrate on helping someone else. God is going to use you, even in captivity.

Jeremiah implied that God's time was not Israel's time. His reference to "seventy years" certainly had historical significance for them. But more, it had a "fullness-of-time," an "in-God's-time," a "when-God-gets-good-and-ready" connotation that marks the quality of a relationship between

God and God's people. It was saying, "After seventy years, when you've repented for trying to do it your way, when you've been able to affirm that there is no other God like the God of Israel, when your priests and prophets have turned their hearts to me, I will visit you and fulfill my promise to you and bring you back to this place." It was a word with purpose! There were lessons to be learned in Babylon.

In our own lives Babylon will occur. There will be times when our estrangement from God will lead us to places of spiritual soul searching and pondering. For us, Babylon is not a place, but rather an experience or quality of existence that defines our relationships with God. We've got to go to Babylon. There is no shortcut to our commitment, no stops along the way for our spiritual stamina, no fumbling around with our faith. This is serious business! We must go to Babylon! There will always be those who prefer the shortcut to faithfulness. They neither walk the walk nor talk the talk, but rather excuse themselves, because, after all, there are a whole lot of sinners right in the church. There are those who would convince you that this is not God's plan for you, that you can have peace and prosperity without going through all the discomfort and uneasiness that you may be experiencing in your "Babylonian Bayou." But if we really want to appreciate Jerusalem and get back home spiritually, we must go to Babylon.

Stay in Babylon. I'm convinced that God has an upside-down theology! If we want to be reconciled to God, we've got to suffer sometimes. If we want the sunshine, we've got to go through a little rain. If we want to be strong, we've got to go to some weakening places. If we want to get closer, we've got to experience some estrangement. If we want to rejoice, we've got to shed a few tears. Stay in Babylon!

This word for the weary was not only a word that signifies God's purpose for our lives, but it is a powerful word of *promise*. Listen to the Word of God from the lips of Jeremiah:

> "When seventy years are completed for Babylon, I will come to you and fulfill my gracious promise to bring you back to this place. For I know the plans I have for you . . . plans to prosper you and not to harm you, plans to give you hope and a future. Then you will call upon me and come and pray to me, and I will listen to you. You

will seek me and find me when you seek me with all your heart. I
will be found by you," declares the LORD, "and will bring you back
. . . to the place from which I carried you into exile."
(Jeremiah 29:10-14, NIV)

These beautiful and poetic words of promise remind Israel that God
has not forgotten and never will forget her. For after her time had been
accomplished, the promise of restoration was sure. What a word for
some weary exiles! What a word for some tired children of God! What
a word for those sinking in the low lands of languishing! What a word
for those drowning in the depths of despair!

God said, "You will be a mighty nation. I will give you not just a future,
but a future and a hope. You may have been a mockery among other
nations before, but after seventy years your neighbors will testify that
there isn't any god like Israel's God. You may have tried to design and
define your own heritage, but your plans need to become my plans. You
thought I would forget you in Babylon, but I will gather you from all the
places I have scattered you and bring you back home."

And the promise continues. God said, "*Then*, after you've come to
know me in a new way, after you've put aside your own inclinations
toward infidelity, after you've recommitted yourself to my cause, after
you've allowed me to order your steps, after you've prayed that I would
be pleased with your praise, then when you call me, seek me, and pray to
me I will hear you. When you seek me with your whole heart I will be
found of you." What a word of promise!

In God's own time, he grants that the sufferings of this present time are
consumed with the joy of knowing that he never forsakes his own. You
and I have the blessed assurance in knowing that all things work according to the plan of the eternal and that no matter what we are going
through, we need only remember that God has not forgotten us. The battle is not ours; it's the Lord's. We can't afford to forfeit what God has for
us by leaving Babylon too soon, for only after seventy years can we experience the blessings of the "then" existence. We've got to wait until the
weariness of our existence finds hope in the proleptic "then." We can live
in Babylon as long as there is a "then." What a word for the weary!

This message to the exiles reminds us that God never leaves us without hope. In the midst of our alienation God always comes to us. Jeremiah's "then" leaped over some forty and two generations and got wrapped up in a "now." Now God has come to us in person, a Word in the flesh, a Word for us weary travelers. Now God has come to us through the sacrificial death of Jesus on a rugged cross called Calvary and a hill called Golgotha. God has made good on a promise of restoration. In Jesus, God killed death on the cross and allowed your Lord and mine to rise up with all power in his hands. Now God says, "I know the plans I have for you. You have a future and a hope. When you call me I will answer. When you seek me and pray to me I will hear you. When you seek me with your whole heart I will be found of you. Now," God says, "there is a place I've prepared for you. It's the camp land in New Jerusalem. So walk together, children, don't you get weary. Sing together, children, don't you get weary. Pray together, children, don't you get weary in Babylon. There's a great camp-meeting in the Promised Land."

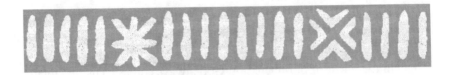

The Declaration of Forgiven Disciples

BY LISA ROXANNE HARRIS

He saith unto him the third time, "Simon, son of Jonas,
lovest thou me?" . . . He said unto him,
Lord, thou knowest all things; thou knowest that I love thee.
Jesus saith unto him, "Feed my sheep."
(John 21:17)

Peter wasn't the only one who heard the question. Others were standing by the shore: Thomas, Nathanael, James and John, and two others also. By virtue of the testimony of the Scripture, in my sanctified imagination, I seem to hear an invitation to stand at the shore and consider what this encounter means to me and my faith. I invite you to join me, to consider my thoughts, perhaps even our thoughts, as we together are bystanders to this encounter with Jesus that took place 2,000 years ago.

We were standing there when Jesus questioned Peter. We watched Peter lower his eyes to the sand. We heard the question-and-answer discussion that was repeated three times. Surely, Peter was confused, but he still listened to the Lord. With only a look we could see it, and we could hear the forgiveness in Jesus' voice. A few more words were spoken, and then, as quickly and mysteriously as Jesus had appeared, he was gone. We were left standing on the shore, Peter's clothes still damp from his jump in the sea. Our physical hunger was satisfied by the meal Jesus had prepared, but our minds and hearts were empty of answers, still filled with much uncertainty. Yet in spite of the uncertainty about what the future might hold, with the resurrection of Jesus our hopes were resurrected. His death was an unexpected detour to our dreams, but now we couldn't help but believe that everything would be all right, because Jesus was alive. He didn't abandon us, even though we had abandoned him.

The trial, sentence, and crucifixion of Jesus were more than we could bear. We all ran. Peter still couldn't believe he had actually denied Jesus three times. None of us can believe the betrayal of Judas. I had denied Jesus also. I didn't say that I wouldn't, but I can't believe the way I ran and hid. (I am sorry Judas Iscariot missed this opportunity to experience this forgiveness—was his betrayal any different than our denial?)

I realize now what I didn't realize as Jesus was making his way to Calvary. In the last several months, I was paying so much attention to how my relationship with him was promoting my popularity. He kept saying, "Follow me. Follow me." And we did. We were ready to follow him right into the palace. I was proud of myself because I thought I was doing so much for him. But I now realize that he was asking for more than I was ready to give. He was asking for total surrender and complete allegiance—he was inviting us to become like him! I cannot believe we asked Jesus where we would sit with him in his kingdom. Peter was not the only one who was trying to impress Jesus—trying to give all the right answers. We were daydreaming about prestige and power. But Jesus was not calling us to be perfect; he was calling us to follow him in the perfect way, and now we know that part of following him means feeding his sheep. I thank the Lord for giving us a second chance. If Jesus asked the question of me, I would offer the same response as Peter.

We cannot help but love the Lord. We were there when Jesus healed Peter's mother-in-law and raised Lazarus from the dead. We were there when Jesus said to the raging sea and the wind, "Be quiet!" and called the demons out of the possessed. We were there when he recognized the sacrificial gift of the woman with two coins and ate meals with those whom others rejected. He washed our feet! He was so patient through our misunderstanding, and he died on the cross for us. He forgave us. How could we not love him? We grew to love Jesus as brother, teacher, friend, healer, promise-keeper, Messiah. And when he appeared to us on the beach, it did not take us long to realize that the life of faith is more about relationships than rules and regulations. I wasn't ready before, but now I am ready to feed his sheep.

As I look here on the sand, I see the fish Jesus helped us to catch—153 to be exact. My God! Jesus fed 5,000 people with 5 loaves of bread and 2 fish. We could feed the *world* with all the fish here!

I know there is more to this charge to feed than food, but I can't help but notice that people seem to pay better attention to a message when their stomachs are full. People believe we care when we listen to them. No, the physical food will not satisfy forever, and any shelter we build is vulnerable to wind and rain. Any clothes we offer will eventually wear away. But all of these acts of faith are important if they draw people to Jesus Christ. We will feed the sheep with everything he has given us. Everything we do we will do in his name. We are completely dependent on Jesus.

We asked Jesus to teach us how to pray; now we must daily ask him how to feed his sheep. Jesus, show us how to feed your sheep. Show us how to feed your sheep who are like the Pharisee, Nicodemus, who grew up in the synagogue but was a babe in matters of faith. Show us how to feed your sheep who are like the woman who was bent over for eight years, focused on her feet and the ground, but who needed to focus her eyes on you. Show us how to feed your sheep who are like the little children others tried to keep away from you. I imagine the little ones are those among the easiest to feed; if only people would not overfeed them with the things they don't need. Show us how to feed your sheep who are like Martha—perhaps so busy trying to impress you that they don't take time to know you. Show us how to feed your sheep who are prone to wander. Show us how to feed your sheep who are like those gathered in the multitude, who want to experience the blessings but do not want to be pressed into serving. Show us how to feed the sheep who are like Simon of Cyrene, the one who carried your cross, who was called to carry the burden we all should have been bearing and who was abused because of the color of his skin.

Jesus, Bread of Life, show us how to feed your sheep. Church, are you ready to feed his sheep as a response to your love for the Lord? Wait!

Before you answer, let me show you something. If you see this passage in Greek you will notice that Jesus asks the question with the word *agape* two times, and each time Peter responds with the word *philos*. The third time Jesus lessens the intensity of the love and uses the same expression for love as Peter does—*philos*—and Peter responds in kind with *philos*. *Agape*, the unconditional, I-lay-my-life-down-for-you kind of love is met with *philos*: a let-me-share-my-lunch, let-me-buy-you-a-nice-present kind of love. But don't be mad at Peter. In this moment, he cannot answer with the whole abandonment and self-sacrifice that *agape* suggests, but the testimony of his life recorded in Acts lets us know that he in fact responded with great *agape*. Peter, still stinging from his threefold denial of Jesus, did not know if *agape* was in him to give. But it was! Peter laid down his life in *agape* love for Jesus and his sheep. He did not turn back.

Church, are you ready to feed the sheep as your response to your love for the Lord? Wait! Before you answer, let me help you overcome your hesitation. When we hear this question, the memory of our denials of Christ may come to mind and we may decide we are not worthy of the work to which God has called us. We remember times when our actions revealed that we had given the wrong answer to the question "What would Jesus do?" Sometimes we will feel like going back, like these disciples who tried to go back to their lives as fishers, but be assured that if you have heard the Lord call once, your life will not be the same. There is no need to go back.

You may be asking, "How can I feed your sheep when I am always hungry?" But it is *because* you know your need and your dependence on the Lord that you are able to be of service for him. It is *because* we recognize our constant need for forgiveness that we are more likely to recognize that need in others. We may fall down, but as long as we sincerely grieve our denial or disobedience, Jesus Christ is always there to pick us up. Don't try to be perfect; just follow him who leads you in the perfect way.

Feeding the sheep may take us to distant places that require passports and planes and visas and vaccinations. Feeding the sheep may require a visit next door or across the street. Feeding the sheep may require paying attention to someone who sits across the table from us at breakfast.

Feeding the sheep will certainly require us to work together and bring together our best resources—best mind, best heart and soul, best energy, and best self—to fulfill God's mission. In essence, when we labor with God and bring together all the good things God has given to us, we are able to feed his sheep and grow the kingdom of God on earth as it is in heaven.

Church, are you ready to feed the sheep as your response to your love for the Lord? By the power of God that is at work in us, by the forgiveness of God that is at work in us, by the love of God that is at work in us, we are able to do what Jesus has asked of us. We are able to feed his sheep. Let's go.

"Lord, we are able, our spirits are thine. Remold us, make us like Thee divine! Thy guiding radiance above us shall be a beacon to God, to love and loyalty."

The Spiritually
Connected Family

BY JACQUELINE E. MCCULLOUGH

*Our Lord Jesus Christ, Of whom the whole
family in heaven and earth is named.*
(Ephesians 3:14-15)

Our society's definition of "family" has over time been redefined, and
it will continue to change. There is no doubt, even without statisti-
cal information, that we are experiencing a lack of intimacy, connection, and endurance in our primary relationships, namely those with
our families. We are concerned about spouse abuse, child abuse, elder
abuse, and student abuse. We are distressed when we watch the news,
read the newspaper, and watch the talk shows that reveal to us the sys-
temic and endemic evils of society that erode our family values and
Christian principles.

The family of today can consist of the traditional mother, father, and
children, but it can also consist of a single parent; one or more extended family members; adopted siblings or foster children; two fathers; two
mothers; and the list goes on. These new configurations have become so
radically different and complicated that our laws lack the ability to
define the legal protection and privileges for the family of the twenty-
first century. It is plain to see that our definition of "family" has changed
significantly.

Jesus also drastically redefined the family in his day. It is remarkable
to know that he was viewed with great suspicion because of many of

his teachings and declarations about the family. The book of Matthew opens up with a long list of names, the genealogy of Jesus, a family tree consisting of forty-two generations of Jews. It showed that the poor carpenter Joseph from Nazareth, an agricultural area, could trace his ancestry to Israel's royalty, King David, and all the way back to Abraham.

Jesus grew up during the time of the revival of Jewish pride. It was during this time when the Jews were being influenced by Greek culture and attempting to preserve their Jewish identity by adopting names that could be traced back to the times of the patriarchs and the Exodus from Egypt. For example, Mary was the name for Miriam, sister of Moses. Joseph was named after one of the sons of Jacob. Jesus, whose Hebrew name is "Joshua," meaning "he who saves," is a common Jewish name. He was raised in a typical Jewish home and was exposed to the Jewish religion and culture. He was circumcised and blessed on the eighth day (see Luke 2:21-34) and was bar-mitzvahed at the age of twelve (see Luke 2:41-46). Then he went home "and was subject unto them: but his mother kept all these sayings in her heart. And Jesus increased in wisdom and stature, and in favour with God and man" (Luke 2:51-52). After this, the curtain falls on Jesus' personal life and very little is known about this historical Christ and his family life, except that his father was a carpenter and that they lived in Nazareth.

When Jesus left home and began to live out his purpose, there was no mention of his family. Was he anti-family, or was he about to redefine the family? If so, within what context? Our society has outlined the structure of the family within a social-cultural context and generally premised it on a secular, humanistic point of view. Jesus, however, determined the nature of the family in a spiritual context:

> While he yet talked to the people, behold, his mother and his brethren stood without, desiring to speak with him. Then one said unto him, Behold, thy mother and thy brethren stand without, desiring to speak with thee. But he answered and said unto him that told him, Who is my mother? and who are my brethren? And he stretched forth his hand toward his disciples, and said, Behold my mother and my brethren! For whosoever shall do the will of my

Father which is in heaven, the same is my brother, and sister, and mother. (Matthew 12:46-50)

While Jesus was teaching, some of his disciples interrupted him and alerted him to the presence of his mother and brothers (half-brothers). Was Jesus so anointed and so powerful that he wanted to disregard his mother and brothers?

The sense of the text is centered on Jesus' purpose and priority. At the time when he fully walked into his assignment, Jesus knew that his family would be affected. He was not repudiating his earthly family, because in John 19:26-27, we see Jesus caring for his mother at the cross. What he was doing was emphasizing the supremacy and eternity of his spiritual relationships. He was the God-man, and even his own family would need him to save them from their sins. He understood that his relationship with his heavenly Father far outweighed his relationship with his earthly family, especially if they were not doing or obeying the will of God. A dear friend of mine preached one Good Friday, and her theme was "Blood is thicker than water, but spirit is thicker than blood." This is the essence of Jesus' conviction when it comes to the special bond that is created between spiritual sisters and brothers, which may never necessarily occur in a biological family.

We have so many case studies of family crimes, family hatred, family discord, family turmoil, and family disintegration. There must be something greater to hold the family together than what we are applying in our relationships. The answer is Jesus' approach to family. If there is a common belief system, or worldview, within a family, then there is a bond beyond feeling, status, success, accomplishments, ego, competition, and all other issues which can cause conflict. The common denominator is Jesus. Jesus is the glue and the adhesive that holds together different people with different feelings, ideas, and needs. The Master Teacher may appear to be antagonistic toward the family unit, but it is the wisdom and spirit of his teachings that will bring cohesiveness to the family.

The paradoxical teachings of Jesus can be very troublesome to the natural or carnal mind. For example, in Matthew 10:34-37, we read:

Think not that I am come to send peace on earth . . . but a sword. For I am come to set a man at variance against his father, and the daughter against her mother, and the daughter in law against her mother in law. And a man's foes shall be they of his own household. He that loveth father or mother more than me is not worthy of me: and he that loveth son or daughter more than me is not worthy of me.

This text has been used and misused to depict Jesus' voice against the family. This is not a voice against family, but a voice against the man or woman who cannot take a stand to live for Christ because of family pressure or commitment. Jesus is declaring emphatically that one's loyalty to Christ is preeminent above all other earthly relationships.

This is not to say that one must not relate, communicate, or have dealings with family or have family responsibilities. What it does suggest is that if any family member decides to live for Christ and the other family members do not accept Christ, there may be conflict and disruption in the relationship. There are countless testimonies of people who are or were vigorously persecuted and excommunicated from family because of their stand for Christ. Jesus was right in saying that if our commitment to him is not far above our commitment to family, then we are not worthy of him and will not be able to stand the pressure of being identified with him.

The redefinition has to do with a family being truly a family both biologically and spiritually. Jesus' words in Matthew 12:46-48 must have sounded strange and irksome to a community attempting to maintain its ancestry and identity. He probably sounded extremely anti-tradition by publicly disowning and disregarding his mother and brothers. Jesus did not deny, however, that these were his earthly family members. He merely went beyond the portals of the secular understanding of family and took it to another realm. This realm is spiritual family connection. This new "family" includes anyone who does the will of the Father in heaven. Jesus' statement indicates that a family can only be a real family if the members live to please God. If all of the biological families or spiritual members of the family of God live to please God, then these will be families that will pray together, live together, grow together, and stay together.

Jesus' redefinition of "family" is so "anti" the world and, sad to say, "anti" some of our "churchy" concepts of life and family. Our society's redefinition of family is far from reflecting what truly connects and binds us together as a unit. We must learn to faithfully hold on to the promise that Paul, the apostle, gave to the jailor when he asked, "Sirs, what must I do to be saved? And they said, Believe on the Lord Jesus Christ, and thou shalt be saved, and thy house" (Acts 16:30-31). It is evident from this passage that we have a promise of household salvation and that we must stand in the gap until this promise is appropriated to our homes and families. It is then and only then that we can truly say that we are a "spiritually connected family."

Sisters in the Right Place at the Right Time

BY CAROLYN TYLER GUIDRY

*And who knoweth whether thou art come to the kingdom
for such a time as this? . . . And so will I go in unto the king,
which is not according to the law: and if I perish, I perish.*
(Esther 4:14,16)

One of the most interesting stories in the whole Bible is the story of Esther, a beautiful young child who was suddenly transformed from a graceful, carefree girl into a woman. She was plunged unannounced into the crossfire of imperial politics and a predicament of supposed powerlessness. The setting of the story is the kingdom of Persia, and Esther enters the tale after a strange prelude involving King Ahasuerus and Queen Vashti.

King Ahasuerus was very prosperous, and he celebrated it with a total of five months of eating and drinking with his provincial governors. He then concluded with an "open house" party that lasted for seven days! In all of this time he never invited his number-one wife, Queen Vashti, to join him. No, not one time. A royal husband invited his associates to party with him for a hundred and eighty-seven days and never even invited his wife! That is, never until he was drunk, stoned, high on wine. Then, abruptly, he ordered his wife to come in so he could show off her striking beauty.

When he sent a summons for her to appear, she sent a note back saying, "I'm not coming!" I can just imagine sister Vashti indignantly stiffening her neck and putting her hands on her hips and saying, "You didn't invite me before, while you did all this partying and showing off, so you just go on with your party." As a parting shot, she probably told him, "As a matter of fact, I got a party of my own going on. My girls and I are having a good time. So no, I am not coming!"

Now the nobles of the kingdom became a little concerned. If the queen is allowed to disrespect the king in this manner, this thing just might become contagious, and the rest of the women in the kingdom might get some foolish ideas. They might get the notion that *they* can be disobedient, too. I can hear the men grumbling, "We have a problem! The king has to put Vashti in her place." And so, to teach her to stay in what they thought was a "woman's place," and to make her an example to *all* women, King Ahasuerus divorced and demoted Queen Vashti. Then, following the advice of his sages, he launched a kingdom-wide search for a new queen.

That brings us to the young maiden Esther's entry into the tale. She was an orphan Jewess, living in exile in the kingdom with her cousin Mordecai, who had virtually adopted her. When Mordecai learned of the royal search for a new queen, he determined to enter Esther into this search, which amounted to a beauty contest as far as qualifications were concerned.

Swearing his lovely charge, Esther, to secrecy about her ethnic background, cousin Mordecai groomed her for the role of queen. Then he brought Esther before the king to join the throng of young women vying to become the new queen. As it turned out, "the maiden pleased him [the king]" (Esther 2:9). In fact, he grew to really love Esther, and he lavished riches and servants on her. But he just was so busy that he could go as long as thirty days without even laying his eyes on her dazzling loveliness.

Esther was now the number-one wife. But even though Mordecai was a court officer, he deemed it wise not to be openly associated with Esther. It might blow his game. He would have enjoyed personally witnessing her luxurious lifestyle, but he communicated with her only through trusted servant messengers.

It was wise that Mordecai did this, because he had a powerful enemy named Haman, who was the king's chief aide. Haman hated Mordecai so much that he deceived the king into signing a genocidal order that *all* the Jews be massacred. When Mordecai heard of this royal decree, he sent a note to Esther urging her to use her influence with the king to save her people. It was a risky business, and Esther told him so in her written response. She reminded him that she hadn't been called to come in to the king for thirty days. If she took it on herself just to barge into his presence, she could be sentenced to death.

When Mordecai learned of Esther's hesitation, he sent her a second note. He warned her, "If thou altogether holdest thy piece at this time, then shall there enlargement and deliverance arise to the Jews from another place; but thou and thy father's house shall be destroyed: and who knoweth whether thou art come to the kingdom for such a time as this?" (4:14). Mordecai was warning Esther that Haman had the authority and the governmental mobilization to carry out this bloody decree. He would stop at nothing to exterminate *all* Jews. This included not only Mordecai, but Esther and all her relatives as well. She need not think she could escape.

In the word that Esther sent back to her adoptive father, Mordecai, she first asked all her believing Jewish sisters and brothers to engage in three days and nights of prayer and fasting, and she promised that she and her maidens would do the same. The text says that "there was great mourning among the Jews, and fasting, and weeping, and wailing; and many lay in sackcloth and ashes" (4:3). And now Esther also put aside her luxuries and finery to commit herself to prayer and fasting for three days. Those luxuries the king had given her were wonderful! Dressing up was delightful! But she had to remember that there was a world beyond luxury that was dying for her immediate attention. Nothing was more important.

Then followed the words of commitment which have rung down through the centuries: "And so will I go in unto the king, which is not according to the law: and if I perish, I perish" (4:16).

We, too, are called to give our very lives over to be used by God to meet the needs of today's needy and oppressed. We cannot afford to be a part of the silent majority. As fervently as we pray, we need also to speak out in action so others can hear. We need to pray and then act under God's direction. We have to pray without ceasing and be about our duty of witnessing and lifting up the name of Jesus.

Sisters, we have been called, yes, for a time such as this! If not now, when? If not you, who? We are not saved to wait for the hereafter, but to be responsible for those around us here and now. The great need today is that the world be led to Jesus Christ. I know that this is not a popular topic of conversation, but Jesus is still what the world needs. If you and I don't lift up his name, many in the places where we live and serve will not come to know Jesus before they leave this planet.

It is not enough that "me and mine" are saved. We are called to be genuinely concerned that the whole world should know this Christ whose name we bear. That world includes the victims of the Hamans of the drug trade and the lepers, so to speak, of the HIV affliction. This lost world of sickness and distress, as the song says, "will know that we are Christians by our love." That kind of living will again become the testimony of Christians everywhere. My sisters, there is a need for believers to become totally involved in responding to the world's cries for help, both spoken and unspoken. We must strive to assure that there never again will be a Columbine tragedy to commemorate or a September 11 to make us afraid. We must be so involved in the world that never again will our babies be found in dumpsters or our children beaten and battered to death or lost so that nobody knows where they are. Until racism, sexism, violence, and corruption become bad memories rather than stark reality, we are called to be determined to make a difference in the world. The messages to us from on high challenge us to cause changes so that our children will no longer have to turn to drugs for comfort. We are called to transform our classrooms and playgrounds from battlegrounds to parks of peace.

My sisters, we are called to be like Esther, to obediently settle into the places where God puts us, at the time when we are needed to serve, if we are to meet the needs of today's world. Yes, Christian women, like Esther we are living in perilous times, but we are also living in glorious, exciting times. Are we doing what our Lord expects to find us doing when he comes? Are we feeding the hungry, clothing the naked, housing the homeless, loving the children, lifting up Jesus' name? Why are we here? What have we come to do this time? What are we doing in the kingdom? What are we doing for God's sake? What are we doing in God's name? What is our task? Perhaps it is to bind up the brokenhearted, to preach good news to the poor and to give sight to the blind. Sisters, we are in the right place at the right time. Make sure you make the most of your position in the kingdom of God! Amen!

In the face of death itself, Esther sounds a subtle note of triumph. My inspired imagination hears her shouting forth, "If I perish doing what I came to this kingdom for in the first place, then glory to God!" Esther had found her place in life. She had discovered why God made her and placed her in this pivotal place of influence. She had found out where she belonged, and she now realized that to be alive and active in the very will of God was worth more than life itself. "If I perish in the kingdom in such a time as this, I perish!" Amen!

It's a Good Thing!

BY JO ANN BROWNING

And we know that all things work together
for good to them that love God, to them who
are the called according to his purpose.
(Romans 8:28)

There are times when we need the Lord to speak a little word of encouragement to us. Every once in a while it is good to let the Lord take our spiritual temperatures, to make sure we are spiritually intact, so we can keep on pressing toward the mark of the higher calling in God. I say so because many Christians seem to be fascinated with a quick-fix theology, looking for the easy way out. They don't want to go through anything. They can't be committed for the long haul. They seem to seek things that promise five principles for this, three steps for that, do this to get that.

Instead, my sisters and my brothers, we need to trust God while we are waiting through trial. We must ask God right now to awaken within us a certainty whenever we are uncertain. Like you, I also struggle. I come before you still wondering about our President and his cohorts, who seem to lead in such a way that we hear one thing and yet sense in our spirits that something else is really going on. I wonder when I hear of thousands unemployed. I know who those people will be—if we are in the labor pool at all. When I hear of all this I feel like throwing in the towel, but I have to trust the Lord anyhow. Why? Because it is not over until God says it's over. God has the final word. *And it's a good thing.*

That is what Paul is saying to us in his letter to the church at Rome. He is speaking to us of what he has been through and telling us of the things the Lord did for him personally. Paul speaks candidly from the heart and out of his experiences. Paul, who had been whipped, shipwrecked, stoned, and left to die, declares, in spite of difficulties and disappointments, that "all things work together for good to them that love God, to them who are the called according to his purpose" (Romans 8:28).

We need to know, right now, that as he did for Paul, God is working in whatever we are going through. The ups are working together, and the downs are working together. The good is working together, and the bad is working together. The sickness is working together, and the health is working together. God is working out whatever we are going through— all things! In our families, in our marriages, in problems with our children, in our jobs with our crazy bosses—all things are working together. In the war in Iraq, *all things*; in sons and daughters overseas, *all things*; in massive unemployment, *all things*. In everything we are faced with and concerned about, all things are working together for good. Whatever it looks like, whatever it feels like, in all things through our tears, in all things through our weariness, *all things are working together for good.*

But hear me, Church, Paul is not saying that bad things happen to us for our good. What he is saying is that when they do happen, God reserves the option of working good through them. The focus in the text is on the fact that God is in the midst of *all things*, and because God is God, we can be confident and assured that all things are in his hands. We are in a win-win situation. And *it's a good thing.*

The only way that we can be assured and confident in times of trouble is to know God for ourselves, to know that we are in a relationship with him through Jesus Christ. We have peace in knowing that the God of Abraham and Sarah, the God of Isaac and Rebecca and Jacob, has it all under control. The same God who got Joseph out of the pit will get us out of our pits. The same God who parted the Red Sea for Moses and Israel, because he loves us and we love him, will part the Red Seas in our lives. It's a good thing that the same God who protected the men in the fiery furnace, the one who locked the lions' jaws for Daniel, is with us when we step into our fiery furnaces. The same Creator who delivered others will deliver us all. *It's a good thing!*

Why? Because there is nothing too hard for God! Those of us who love

God and have been called according to his purposes—from the pulpit to the choir loft to the pews—ought to be glad that we are saved. God wants this whole creation to be totally united with him through Jesus Christ. You see, Church, the paradox of God is that when we have adversities or when there is wickedness, God gets to show his power and might by completely turning around the impossible. In verse 31 Paul asks, "What shall we then say to these things? If God be for us, who can be against us?" So it really doesn't matter who is against us, because ultimately we have victory through Jesus Christ.

Paul could say these things because he had wrestled through to *his* faith. But I have my *own* testimony. My journey includes twenty years of service at Ebenezer A.M.E. Church in Fort Washington, Maryland; twenty-four years of marriage to Pastor Grainger Browning; and experiencing for the first time empty-nest syndrome with both of our children away from home at the same time. I continue to rely on God as I did when I was unemployed, eating with food stamps, without a place to call our own, recovering from the miscarriage of our second child, having run-over shoes and one black suit to wear every Sunday. The tests of faith were everywhere: living with roaches and rats, working three jobs at one time, working on a master's degree and trying to earn a doctorate while working at the church, caring for my family, and substitute teaching at a nearby high school—all at the same time. Sometimes I wondered if God really heard my cry. Sometimes I questioned myself and wondered if I had really heard from God. Sometimes I could not believe the overloads and complications that I found myself in. But I have come to tell you this morning that I know, that I know, that I know, that I know, that I know that *it's a good thing*. God was squeezing out a good thing—a blessing—while I went through all of those things. I know now that all things work together for good for those who love God and are called according to his purpose. If I had never had problems, I wouldn't know that God could solve them. If I had given up way back then, I would have missed the blessing of serving as copastor at Ebenezer. Thanks be to God for a reasonable portion of health and a mind not afflicted, for our children in college and not in prison, and friends who love and care for us.

In verse 33, Paul tells us that in the midst of all the things we will come up against as Christians, we should remember that God justifies, so we need not fear. And in verse 34, Paul tells us that we do not have to worry because Jesus the Christ is sitting at the right hand of God interceding on our behalf. Yes, the enemy may be on our trail trying to discourage us, disappoint us, or destroy us. The enemy may even be trying to make us question whether God will come through for us. But, I want you to know without reservation, without doubt, without fear, without second-guessing, that whatever we are going through, it won't last forever. And in the end it is working itself out for our good. Hold on; don't give up; know it's a good thing and that God really knows and cares. Let's put our faith and our trust in the almighty God, who will bring us through. *It's a good thing.* For "if God is for us, who can be against us" (NIV)?

Paul ends with reiterating that because God is who God declares he is, and because all things are working together for our good, it's a good thing. Paul ends with a confidence and an assurance that the saints of God, we the saved, are more than conquerors through God who loves us (see Romans 8:37). We are more than conquerors because of what Jesus did on the cross. He suffered, bled, and died. When he went to the grave and got up on the third day full of power, he gave us the confidence, the assurance, and the *victory* in the battle of life. So it's a good thing.

You need to know, in the midst of it all, that God has your back. It's a good thing to know that nothing is able to separate us from the love of God, which is in Christ Jesus. It's a good thing that, like Paul, we are persuaded. I don't know about you, but I need to remain persuaded in the midst of trials and tribulations, questions and doubts, fears, issues, and concerns. In sickness, be persuaded; in doctor reports, be persuaded. It's a good thing that neither death, nor life, nor angels, nor principalities, nor things present, nor things to come, nor height or depth, nor any other creature shall be able to separate us from the love of God through Christ Jesus (8:38-39, author's paraphrase). It's a good thing.

It's a good thing that he saved my soul and made me whole. It's a good thing that he loves me. It's a good thing that he is my battle-ax. It's a good thing that he is my shield. It's a good thing that he is my sword. It's a good thing that he is my hope. It's a good thing that when I was hungry he fed me. It's a good thing that when I was lonely he comforted me. It's a good thing that when I had no place to rest my head he made a way. It's a good thing that "my hope is built on nothing less than Jesus' blood and right-eousness." It's a good thing. It's a good thing that "the LORD is my shep-herd; I shall not want" (Psalm 23:1). He's my doctor in the hospital. He's my lawyer in the courtroom. He's my all in all. It's a good thing, it's a good thing, and I feel all right. It's a good thing, I feel like going on. It's a good thing. It's a good thing. It's a good thing. *It's a good thing!*

Can Any Good Thing Come out of Nazareth?

BY AUDREY BRONSON

*And Nathanael said unto him, Can there any good thing come out
of Nazareth? Philip saith unto him, Come and see.*
(John 1:46)

In John 1:43-46 we see Jesus beginning to assemble a group of men who would become his disciples. Everything was going fine. He got Andrew—no problem. Andrew found Peter—no problem. Philip came on board—no problem. But then things hit a snag when Philip tried to convince Nathanael to join them. When Nathanael heard that Jesus was from Nazareth, he got an attitude and said, "Can any good thing come out of Nazareth?" (1:46, author's paraphrase).

When you meet someone or when you apply for a job, one of the first things people want to know is where you live. What city or neighborhood do you come from? Because certain neighborhoods and cities have reputations. In other words, people can base their opinions of you on where you live.

Let's take a look at Nazareth. The town was utterly insignificant. There is no mention of it in the Old Testament, the Talmud, or the Midrash (early Hebrew writings), or in any pagan contemporary writings. It was akin to Jesus' birth in a stable. It was a most unlikely, nothing sort of town. It was the ghetto, not a place where people thought a messiah would be born. No wonder, then, that Nathanael asked, "Can any good thing come out of Nazareth?"

The people of Nazareth were in darkness, and even they could not see that their hometown boy was somebody special. They tried to kill him; they were jealous. It is to be noted that the demons knew who Jesus was, but the people did not. Of course, a prophet is not without honor save in his own country (see Matthew 13:57, Mark 6:4).

Jesus is proof that where you come from is not really that important. It is where you are going that matters. There are twenty-five or thirty references in the Scriptures that refer to Jesus being from Nazareth. That tells me that you can be in the slums, but the slums do not have to be in you. You see, Nazareth did not make Jesus; instead, *Jesus* put *Nazareth* on the map.

Let's compare Jesus and Paul. Look at Acts 21:37-39. Paul was from Cilicia's capital city of Tarsus. He wouldn't be afraid to let you know where he was from. He was proud of his hometown. Tarsus was renowned as a place of education. Its citizens were proud of their philosophers. It had an important university and literary schools that were world-class. It was cultured and proud of its Greek culture. Tarsus was prosperous, an important trading place, and it had gathered a colony of Jews who grew prosperous in this city of considerable consequence.

Paul was one of those Jews. But upon his encounter with Jesus in Acts 22:8, Paul asked, "Who art thou, Lord?" Jesus answered, "I am Jesus of Nazareth." In other words, the boy from Tarsus had to bow to the boy from Nazareth—the ghetto. This shows us that Jesus can take nothing and make something out of it.

Some folks think of the left as "the other hand," not as good as the right. No one wants to be *left* out or *left* back. Everyone wants to be *right*, to be in their *right* minds, in the *right* place at the right time, to be ceremoniously seated at the *right* hand of the host or hostess at a banquet table. The right is the side of protocol. Right wingers are on the conservative side. The left side is the minority, the remnant, the remainder. As a matter of fact, there are more than 100 biblical references to the right hand but only 10 or less to the left hand. The left side is the residue and, yes, even the refuse.

But when Job was searching for God, he went forward but he could not find God; he went backward, but he could not find God; but then he looked to the left, and there was God. When Patrick Henry, Martin Luther of Germany, and Martin Luther King of Alabama stood up, the house may have gotten uneasy, but God began to work. The left side is the side of creativity and critical change. It is the case, sometimes, that the person who is lost in the crowd is the means through which God works. Take, for example, the woman with the issue of blood, a woman with the odds against her, who managed to touch the hem of Jesus' garment. He proclaimed, "Somebody touched me!" and right away the fountain of her blood dried up (see Luke 8:45-47). The so-called weaker vessel became the willing vessel. A Mary McLeod Bethune, a Mother Teresa, a Harriet Tubman was set free. The left-outs were put in the right place by the hand of God, which works on the left side.

We could say that Nazareth is on the left. The people in the synagogue at Nazareth got uneasy when Jesus stood up and said, "The Spirit of the Lord is upon me, because he hath anointed me to preach the gospel to the poor; he hath sent me to heal the brokenhearted, to preach deliverance to the captives, and recovering of sight to the blind, to set at liberty them that are bruised, to preach the acceptable year of the Lord" (Luke 4:18-19). Jesus came into his own world through the back door, on the left side of society, and allowed himself to be born in an animal stall, wrapped in swaddling cloths and laid in a manger. Throughout his entire ministry he identified with the weak side of society—the put down, the left out, and the leftovers. He knew that sometimes it is David going up against the giants of society with five small stones and the power of the Lord God Jehovah in the slingshot that achieves powerful results. He knew that the left side was the most unpredictable side, the place where God does his work.

But no one thought any good thing could come out of Nazareth.

Allow me to tell you what is happening in our Nazareth in Philadelphia, where I live. When we move in, other folks move out; then they call it a ghetto. When we move in, city services to Nazareth go down; unemployment hits us to a greater degree. As a result, houses get boarded up and drugs are sold for income. Can any good thing come out of Nazareth? Businesses close down; high-priced check cashing businesses replace banks. They have written us off, saying, "Nothing good can come out of the 'hood." But we are having a revival in the ghetto.

Everyone and everything leaves our Nazareth but the Church, and because the Church is there, that means Jesus is still there, still making a banquet out of two little fishes and five loaves of bread. Jesus is still there making a way out of no way, building up the torn down—torn-down neighborhoods, torn-down lives. He is making cathedrals out of store-fronts. He is giving hope to the hopeless. He is raising up the left-down, bringing in the left out, and making something beautiful out of the left-overs. Something good is happening in Nazareth.

A minister once told the story of taking his children to the beach one day. They noticed newly hatched baby turtles struggling to get out from under the sand (turtles lay their eggs in the sand). The turtles' destination was the sea. The children felt sorry for the baby turtles and proceeded to help some of them by picking them up and putting them in the ocean. These baby turtles were soon devoured by the denizens of the sea. But the turtles that were allowed to continue the struggle and make it to the sea on their own strength—these were the ones who survived in the sea, for the strength they needed to survive was gained in their struggle. We will make it because we are strong. We are strong because our strength is in our struggle and our help comes from God.

Our 'hood, our Nazareth, looked hopeless, but it gave birth to some who are dedicated to rebuilding in the name of Jesus. They are giving back to their Nazareths. Good things are coming out of the ghetto, by the power of the ghetto child of Nazareth and the amazing grace of God. And these good things are resurrecting West Philadelphia. Can anything good come out of Nazareth? Yes, in God's time and with God's power and control, it can! Hallelujah! Amen!

A Journey of Blind Faith

BY LILLIE LAWTON TRAVIS

*By faith Abraham . . . went out, not
knowing whither he went.*
(Hebrews 11:8)

The call of God is not a stagnant experience or an end in itself. It is an ever-unfolding new journey of faith. It is an adventure characterized by mobility, in which God takes us from where we are and leads us to where he wants us to be. It starts in time and ends in eternity. It begins the moment when we accept Christ as our Lord and Savior and continues until we hear him say, "Well done."

All of God's children have received at least three divine calls. The first call is the call to salvation. Those who receive this call are delivered or set free from sin. The second call is the call to discipleship, in which we are asked to follow God's will in our lives, through the study of Jesus in God's Word and through prayer and preparation. The third call is the call to service, or ministry, empowered and guided by God. Those who receive this call cheerfully and sacrificially serve God and humankind.

The call of God is not gender-specific. God is no respecter of persons, accepting male and female alike and accepting whoever will respond to his loving embrace and impartial, steadfast command. It involves pain and sacrifice at times. Paul says that all who are led by the Spirit of God are children of God, which is another way of expressing the call (see Romans 8:14). And so we are heirs of God and joint-heirs with Christ if we share in his suffering.

The writer of Hebrews made a similar observation about the call of faith when referring to Abraham as one of the pilgrims of faith.

84

A Journey of Blind Faith

Abraham's journey of faith led him from familiar and comfortable surroundings in Ur of the Chaldees to the land of Canaan. He embarked upon a trusting relationship with God, indicated by the change in his name from Abram (meaning "exalted father") to Abraham (meaning "father of many nations"). The suffering and risk of the journey to which he was called is summed up in the words of our text: He knew not "whither he went."

The apostle Paul not only refers to Abraham as the father of many nations, but also as the father of the faithful. Thus is recorded the ultimate realization of God's promise that Abraham would become a blessing to the people of God.

At the age of seventy-five, Abram set out from Haran with his wife Sarai, his nephew Lot, and all his possessions and servants. He arrived safely in the land of Canaan some time later. Leaving Haran was a great leap of faith. He must have had some serious reservations about leaving his homeland for a destination unknown. But Abram journeyed on, and God spoke to him, promising to show him the land. It would be the land on which he had been guided to tread, and it would be given to Abram's offspring. Although Abram was advanced in years and had no children of his own, he took God at his word, set aside his personal reservations, and worshiped God by building altars as he went.

After several years of wandering, trying experiences, and childlessness, God appeared to Abram in a vision to bolster his faith and reassure him of the promise. God did this by challenging Abram to scan the skies and count the stars as an indication of the number of his future offspring. Abram obeyed God, and it was credited to him as righteousness. God also restated the promise to give the land of Canaan as a possession to Abram's seed. Abram could not see how God would fulfill such a promise, so he asked for a sign of God's faithfulness. God had Abram bring certain animals to him and ceremonially dissect and offer them. Then at sunset Abram had a dream in which God passed through and foretold the generations. Abram had to acknowledge his own limitations and that God was able to perform what God had said.

Abram's journey of faith took an interesting detour later on in the story, when he was eighty-six years old. His wife convinced him to father a child by her handmaid Hagar. This unwarrantable attempt to assist God in keeping the covenant led to needless pain and awkwardness on the part of Abram, Sarai, Hagar, and later Ishmael, the son.

Abram and Sarai still had no children together, even after he reached the age of ninety-nine, when Sarai was eighty-nine. This was twenty-four years after he had started his walk of faith with God. Therefore, God reaffirmed his covenant with Abram in a more graphic and profound way. God said, "I am God Almighty; walk before me and be blameless. I will confirm my covenant between me and you and will greatly increase your numbers" (Genesis 17:1-2, NIV). Out of great reverence for God, Abram fell on his face, and God reiterated the covenant by once again promising to make Abram the father of many nations.

This was the time when God changed Abram's name to Abraham, and Sarai's name to Sarah, because she would become the mother of nations, and kings of peoples would come from her. God also added to Abraham's duties under the covenant the rite of circumcising every male of his extended household eight days after birth.

Once again Abraham sought to help God fulfill the promise. He believed that Ishmael would be the one through whom the blessing would come. But God repeated to Abraham that he and *Sarah* would bear a son, and that through a son named Isaac the covenant would be fulfilled. In accordance with God's word, to her joyous surprise, Sarah did bear Abraham a son. In keeping with the covenant, they circumcised him on the eighth day. Abraham was 100 and Sarah was 90.

Abraham's journey of faith reached its greatest test when God commanded him to offer up his son Isaac as a human sacrifice on Mt. Moriah. This would destroy Abraham's only hope for an innumerable host of descendants. Yet, without questioning God, Abraham raised his knife, ready by obedient faith to slay his son. Suddenly, an angel of the Lord instructed him to stop and substitute a ram from a nearby bush.

Thus, Abraham passed the test with flying colors. As a result, the angel declared that the Lord would bless Abraham and his descendents and make them as numerous as the stars in the sky. He also announced that through Abraham's progeny, all the nations of the earth would be blessed. Then Abraham returned to his servants, and they set off together for

Beersheba in southern Canaan. In other words, this journey of faith led him geographically from northern to southern Canaan and spiritually from uncommon faith to unswerving commitment to the will of God.

Like Abraham, my own experience with God has been a journey of faith. I accepted Jesus Christ as my Lord and Savior at the tender age of twelve years old. During those growing years, my life was not easy. I was raised in a family of eleven on a farm where money and comforts were scarce. This caused me to yearn to achieve and escape my unpleasant conditions. My prospects were dim, and I was often discouraged. But one Sunday I gave my heart to Jesus. As I grew in the faith I began to cope with my predicament. As the light of faith made my world brighter, I got along better with my sisters and brothers and schoolmates. My faith in God began to increase, which was evidenced in neighborhood affairs and in our home. Bible study, youth choir, and Vacation Church School all planted in me a little more trust in God, and what once seemed a dim and unpromising future brightened up by faith.

My journey of faith led me to matriculate at Cheyney State Teachers College to prepare myself for greater service in the community. During those years, I was a faithful member of the Christian Student Union, where I taught Bible study and led vespers services. Such involvement helped to guide me in making godly decisions and shaped me spiritually. Preparing myself for a teaching career prompted me to relocate to Washington, D.C., where I joined the Salem Baptist Church, taught Sunday school, sang in the choir, and served as assistant church school superintendent. The sacrifices and commitment of these responsibilities helped prepare me for future ministerial service. God's plan for my life was slowly but surely unfolding.

Little did I know that I would later marry the pastor of Salem Baptist Church, who served with distinction for thirty-three years. As the first lady of a busy inner-city congregation, there were many challenges to overcome. God called me into the gospel ministry soon after the death of my husband. This climactic continuation of my journey of faith has led me to divinity schools, where I have received both master's and doctorate degrees.

God's exciting plan for my life is still unfolding. I am still being led into experiences like Abraham's. Not only do I have no notion of whither I am going by God's guidance; I wouldn't even have dreamed of such a personal "Promised Land." The writer of Hebrews has put his finger on the key to surprising abundance of living. It is a faith that trusts God enough to follow the guidance of his Spirit into the unknown. People like Abraham and me can take no credit. We can only praise God's holy name and testify, as did our ancestors when they sang, "I'm on my journey now, an' I wouldn't take nothin' for my journey now."

In these more recent years, my heart sings out constantly the hymn written by black sister Doris M. Akers:

> Lead me, guide me along the way,
> For if you lead me I cannot stray,
> Lord, let me walk each day with Thee,
> Lead me, oh, Lord, lead me.

From Easter to Epiphany to Eternity

BY CHERYL D. WARD

*Forgetting those things which are behind, and reaching forth
unto those things which are before, I press toward the mark
for the prize of the high calling of God in Christ Jesus.*
(Philippians 3:13-14)

I n the motion picture *Boomerang*, starring Eddie Murphy, Halle Berry,
Robin Givens, Eartha Kitt, and many others, we witness the life of a
brother named Marcus Graham (Eddie Murphy). He is a very distin-
guished, debonair corporate executive who plays with, persistently
prances around, derisively denigrates, and impudently imitates love. He
does everything with love except "fall in" love. I pose that the Christian
Church, the body of believers, demonstrates and even replicates Marcus's
behavior on a spiritual level.

We've been "playing" church for many years. We assign someone to be
the preacher and another to be deacon and others to play their roles. We
come to church, but not to Christ. We pay our tithes, but refuse to give
God our time. We serve on boards, committees, auxiliaries, congresses,
and conventions, but neglect to serve God and our fellow humankind.
Yes, we, the people of God, pose a good front by filling sanctuaries, but
unfortunately we miss the mark when it comes to "being the Church."

Easter is the primary occasion when we exemplify this behavior. I am
not trying to point the finger at only the Easter attendees. I'm just merely trying to say that Easter has to be more than a day for ostentatious

outfits, hairdos, and colored eggs. Easter has to become an event that happens, happened, and is happening within each of us.

The name "Easter" derives from the name of the Anglo-Saxon goddess of spring, but the Christian festival developed from the Jewish Passover, because according to the gospel, the events of Jesus' last days took place at the time of Passover. Easter was originally observed on the day following the end of the Passover feast, regardless of the day of the week. In the mid-second century, some Gentile Christians began to celebrate Easter on Sunday, on the fourteenth day into the spring season, with the preceding Friday observed as the day of Christ's crucifixion. Traditionally, Easter was when they would perform water baptism, an outward expression of an inward change.

We must go from Easter being just an event to being an epiphany—a sudden recognition of or insight into meaning, reality, or significance of something. You see, in the aforementioned movie, Marcus Graham played around with love over and over until he came into the meaning, reality, and deep significance of love. His moment of enlightenment came in the scene when he was about to "know" Robin Givens's character (in the biblical sense of the word *know*). They were about to "get it on" when Marcus's conscience got to him. Robin asked him what was bothering him, and he said, "I can't do this, because I'm in love with someone else." She replied, "If you're in love with someone else, then why are you here with me?" He said, "Exactly." He immediately left her and went home to Angela (Halle Berry). But Angela wasn't having it. She said, "Love should've brought your butt home last night." She made him enter into a struggle to restore their relationship.

Marcus realized that the only way to win Angela back was to make a commitment to love. Robin Givens's character may have rocked his world, but Halle Barry's character stole his heart. My favorite scene in the whole movie is right near the end, when Marcus was on his way to win back his woman. There was a bus with a perfume advertisement that his marketing department had produced. It read, "Epiphany, when you know who you love." It was his moment of epiphany.

My question to you today is, "When did you come into the real meaning of knowing the Lord?" When did Easter move from being the day of commemorating Christ's resurrection to a time of understanding that his resurrection needed to take place within you?

Perhaps you're saying that it has not happened to you, but you want to know *how* it can happen. I'm glad you asked that question! In our text, Philippians 3:8-14, the Apostle Paul shares with us how we can have the epiphany experience. He says that first of all we must have a determined purpose to know Christ. He says we must become more deeply and intimately acquainted with him, so that we can perceive, recognize, and understand the wonders of his person more strongly and more clearly. We get to know Christ like we get to know anyone else—by spending time with him. We need to spend quality time in prayer, talking to and hearing from God. The more time we spend with him, the more we get to know his characteristics.

Dr. Gardner Taylor says, "There are some things that happened in our lives, and we have to stand back and look at the situation and say, 'The Lord did that for me.' Sometimes, we have to sit back and say, 'You *go* God!'" When we know God, we recognize things that are of God and things that are not of God. I remember one Sunday morning when Rev. Anthony Williams was singing with the power of the anointing, and I was seated in front of the deaconesses. One of them leaned over to another and said, "That boy is familiar with God." Because she knew God, she knew that power like that only comes from God. She also knew the only way that Rev. Williams could be used by the Holy Spirit like that was if he knew God.

If it means turning off the television sometimes, that's what we have to do. If it means getting off the telephone, that's what we have to do. If it means getting rid of negative people and activities, then that's what we have to do. We need to get to know God.

Dr. J. Alfred Smith says that there are three levels of relationship. *Conversation* is where two people are cordial with one another. They formally greet one another, but they don't share anything intimate. *Communication* is when two individuals are more than mere acquaintances. They can "shoot the breeze, chew the fat." Most of us operate on levels one and two. But few of us reach level three, which is *communion*. At this level, our souls connect. Inner beings co-mingle.

Unfortunately, we often operate at levels one and two with God, without experiencing real communion.

The apostle Paul urges us first to desire, then endeavor to have, and then indulge in intimacy with God. That's why the songwriter could say, "He walks with me and He talks with me and He tells me I'm His own." It is a sweet thing to walk with God.

Then Paul instructs us to learn what it means to suffer, if we are to commune deeply and intimately with God. I'm sorry to relay this bit of information, but a part of intimacy with and commitment to Christ is suffering. Paul says he wants to know Jesus by sharing in his suffering. All of us have to go through some form of a spiritual boot camp. In Spiritual Boot Camp, we will learn how to climb high mountains. We will learn how to walk through low valleys. In Spiritual Boot Camp, we may have to weather a few storms. People may talk about us, but like the old folk said, "You can talk about me as much as you please, but I'm going to talk about you when I'm on my knees." Suffering teaches us to trust in the Lord. Andraé Crouch wrote, "If I never had a problem, I wouldn't know that God could solve them. Through it all, I've learned to trust in Jesus. Through it all, I've learned to trust in God. Through it all, I've learned to depend upon His word."

Paul then shares the good news that even when we suffer, we can experience the power outflowing from Jesus' resurrection. He says that we will be continually transformed in spirit into Christ's likeness. It's an ongoing process. The things that used to upset us don't upset us anymore. The places we used to go, we don't go anymore. The song by Lucie Campbell says, "Something within me that holdeth the reign. Something within me that banishes pain. Something within me I cannot explain. All that I know, there is something within."

The text tells us that when we come to know Christ like this we will experience a moral and spiritual resurrection that will lift us out from among the dead (even while in the body). The moral resurrection means that my mind changes. My thought process is different. The Bible says, "Let this mind be in you, which was also in Christ Jesus" (Philippians 2:5). We are spiritually resurrected when we operate by our spirits. Our minds tell us *what to do*, but our spirits give orders that we *will do it*.

Paul tells us that when we experience this resurrection, it enables us to forget what is behind and press on to what lies ahead. Forgetting what is behind is twofold. It is to forget evils others have done to us, and also to forget the evil things we have done. Jesus tells us that his grace is sufficient (see 2 Corinthians 12:9).

As a minister of the gospel, I do not pretend that this walk is an easy process. I know it gets hard sometimes. There are many days when I come in from the office and I'm weary from the day's activities. I don't want the doorbell or the telephone to ring, because I know it means that somebody wants something. As a general rule, it's someone asking for prayer for their child or a visit for their aging parents. I ask God why I can't even seem to find peace in my own home. I lament to God that home ought to be the one place where I can find peace. I say, "God, why is it that this pastor can't find solitude in her home?" God answers, "Cheryl, you're not home yet! Remember Easter?"

Then I take comfort as my soul sings:

> Beams of Heaven as I go through this wilderness below.
> Guide my feet in peaceful ways. Turn my midnights into days.
> When in the darkness I would grope, Faith always sees a star
> of hope. And soon from all life's grief and dangers, I shall be
> free someday.
> I do not know how long 'twill be, nor what the future holds
> for me.
> But this I know, if Jesus leads me, I shall get home some day.

The Bridge Across the Gap

BY ANGELA WILLIAMS

To every thing there is a season, and a time to every
purpose under the heaven.
(Ecclesiastes 3:1)

As you look around you and celebrate the bountiful season of fall, come along with me on the ol' familiar journey called life, where we witness the uncovering of God's creation along the way. Let's let our imaginations run, if only for a while, and let's direct our attention to the shift in season that is occurring right before our eyes. Let's bring our coats or jackets for such a time as this, for the chill from the brisk wind may sway the trees and chill our spirits along the roadside. As we travel, witness the leaves beginning to take on a new form. The shades of red, gold, and orange give our surroundings new beauty. We see that, yes, every year the seasons change and fall arrives.

This path we are on is not connected with an interstate, nor does it have a name. Some might describe it as a road to nowhere. Perhaps others might say it is lost in a diminutive township or even in a large metropolis. But all who have traveled the path of life before us, with open eyes and hearts, have come to believe that at every point that seemed rutted or invisible there was a bridge across the gaps and a lamp to light the way ahead. So as we embark on this new journey, let us draw closer to God, looking around us and embracing God's work in awe— its artistry and flair. There is a reason and a season for everything, and it all fits and functions together.

The portion of Scripture that describes this phenomenon can be found in Ecclesiastes 3:1-15. Ecclesiastes is one of the wisdom books in the

Bible. Scholars know very little about its author, but the focus of the book is on human nature, and its goal is to guide human beings into the path of meaningful living. In chapter three, verses one through eight, it is apparent that there is an appropriate time for all things, and humans have the responsibility for making right choices. In essence, in God's world of the Spirit, we can receive wise guidance. God will lead us over the gaps if we are walking in the Spirit, but are we interfering with the natural order of things? Are we worrying about the distant, with little or no action in the now?

This summer, after the death of my mother, I found myself traveling, and for the first time in a long time it appeared that I was just going from one bridge over life's gaps to the next. I am not a big admirer of bridges; in fact, when I am crossing them, I feel like gravity is pulling me over. In the same way, in life there are attempts to pull us down at times. During my childhood, I dreamed that I was falling off a bridge. Now that I am more mature, I realize that I was struggling with accepting life's challenges and wanted an easy way out.

Well, it definitely wasn't easy when we were in Savannah recently. My friend and I had to cross a bridge unexpectedly. Previously, we had stopped for directions and were told that we didn't have to take the bridge; instead, we could make a right turn. But just our luck, we ran right into a dead end. We had to cross that bridge anyway; we couldn't turn back. Immediately when we reached the starting point of the bridge, rain started to pour. Little did I realize that it might be part of God's plan to pour down rain on my mental seed during this planting season. How was I to perceive this as a sign that I was about to pull down the shade on the deep sorrow just passed and enter again into the joy of sisterhood?

Just as Scripture tells us, we can be called at any time and in any place. We must be ready both in season and out of what *we* think is season. We know not the hour that God has set, but God has given every hour a purpose. When we allow God into our hearts we can be ready for any bridge.

In the meantime there are a few things we ought to know about bridges. A bridge usually connects roadways and pathways; it can be situated over a body of water, a railroad, another road, or industrial machinery of some kind. According to God's design we are not to make a U-turn on life's bridge. We must confront it, accept it, and find joy even in our discomfort. Whatever the case may be, the bridge of life spans the chasms, the vulnerability, in order to protect us and give us safety.

As you prepare for the bridges in your life, think of what has brought you to this place. Think of some of the circumstances that you have experienced. Then reflect on the tools required for life's journey. There are three parts to God's bridge of life that come to mind.

The first section is called priority. What is important to us? How do we rank our responsibilities? What comes first in our lives? It is easy to get lost or distracted. That is why we must prioritize a variety of good goals and keep each in God's season: projects, family worship, work, etc. Otherwise we get swamped. We may find ourselves struggling when God wants to move us from some good thing out of season. What are our priorities? Does God come first in our lives? Do children matter anymore?

God wants us to enjoy life. When we discover how God sees us, we discover that the real pleasure is found in whatever we have as gifts from God, not in what we accumulate materially. Now that I'm a mom, I see the need to keep our children connected to God. We should be constantly reinforcing God's importance in their lives. The message to them should be that God comes first before anything else. Now is the time to bridge the gap between generations. Now is the time to pass the baton. We have a responsibility to steer our children through the wilderness. We need to assist them into meeting and hearing God in their everyday living. Now is the time to lead them to a bridge across the gap.

The next section of God's bridge is preparation. Anyone can achieve knowledge, but is everyone prepared to make the right turn and go along the path of righteousness? That is why God gives us seasons of preparation. God makes us ready beforehand. God prepares our spirits. God opens our hearts and fills us with purpose. God prepares us by directing us into areas of discomfort. God sends us into strange territory. God travels with us through seasons of both hopelessness and happiness, that we may be prepared. In Christ all experience has both meaning and purpose. God wants to order our steps, because the best is yet to come.

Remember, God's timing is not our timing and some people's preparation periods may be longer than others'. Something may only appear ugly. Sovereign God still makes everyone and everything beautiful in his time. There is a season for everything and a time for every matter under heaven. There is a bridge across every gap.

When we take a concluding look at Ecclesiastes 3:9-15, we become aware of a third section of the bridge, after priority and preparation: God has a *purpose* for all of his creation. Therefore, we all have work to do—purposes to fulfill. Verse two, "a time to plant, and a time to pluck," reminds me of the parable of the wheat and the weeds (see Matthew 13:3-8). A man planted good seed, and in the middle of the night, a stranger planted weeds among the wheat. Both managed to grow together. However, the planter was wise enough to know that at the appropriate time, wheat and weeds could be separated and both could be used for God's purposes. It wasn't easy, but it was God's plan.

God's purposes may require risks and courage from time to time. I am convinced that when Christians move from our comfortable corners and into unmarked territory, we will discover new life. Now is the time to step out into the streets and build up our communities. We need to stand up and encourage those who have fallen victim of the predators and snakes on the highways and byways of wrongdoing. God has not forgotten them. We must put back into society the morals and values of those who came before us.

God has a plan for us that bridges across the gap of any obstacle we may encounter. God gives us the satisfaction of having a place in his plan. When he calls us to do something else, that is a blessing. As we celebrate who we are and what we do each day, let us remember that our purpose in life starts with knowing how God sees and defines us, not how we define one another. Therefore, God wants us to stay connected to him, in constant communication.

One way to practice this is to pray every day. If we would just pray for twenty minutes daily, we would open ourselves up for God to hear our cry and guide us in our purpose for being here. It is like going to a sacred space and putting all our stuff on the table. One thing is for sure: God meets us where we are. We can pull out our dirty laundry and wash it.

We can admit that a sin is a sin and unload our burdens. Then, with God's perfect purposes and timing, we can rejoice at being in the very center of his will. It is the safest and most satisfying place in all the world.

In God's will and purpose, there is no end to our development of new talents, and there is no dull repetition. And we may never see what we shall be in the end. But God brings all our gifts out as we are brought ever closer. Be ye ever glad for what God is planning for our futures. There is a good reason and a season for everything we go through, and there is a bridge across every gap. Praise the Lord!

Anointed for This

BY LEAH E. WHITE

Who knoweth whether thou art come to the kingdom
for such a time as this?
(Esther 4:14)

In the providence of God, you and I are created for a divine purpose. God has a plan for our lives and has anointed and equipped us for our assignments. It was no accident that Harriet Tubman masterminded the Underground Railroad. Nor was it happenstance that Ms. Rosa Parks refused to sit in the back of a Montgomery, Alabama, bus on December 1, 1955. Their choices changed the sensitivity of America to slavery and discrimination. It was not luck that caused Madame Walker to discover the right blend of hair care and beauty-aid products for women of color, giving us a new appreciation for how God created us. Yes, I believe this was all in God's plan!

God told Jeremiah, "For I know the plans I have for you." (29:11, RSV). Neither you nor I have the privilege of living aimlessly. We don't have the luxury of being unproductive. There is no time to be unfocused, and failure is not an option in the plans of God.

One of the main strategies Satan uses to destroy us and our ministries is to create confusion about our personal callings. He aims to keep us from accomplishing what God has placed us here specifically to do. If we are to become all that God desires for us, then each of us must feel driven to fulfill our divine purpose, being confident that we are anointed for it.

Let's look first at an Old Testament model of an anointed woman. One of the most interesting of them all was a young maiden named Esther. She was a Jewish orphan raised by her cousin Mordecai, who was one of the officials of King Ahasuerus of Persia. The drunken king had unceremoniously dethroned Queen Vashti, because she had refused to sacrifice her dignity and dance before his subjects at a ludicrous seven-day drunken party. Angered by Vashti's refusal, the king ordered a gathering of all the young maidens in Sushan to choose a replacement for her. Mordecai brought Esther to the competition, and, to their surprise, she was so beautiful that the king chose her. Mordecai advised Esther never to reveal her Hebrew heritage. She carefully obeyed, since she was painfully aware of their status as exiles in Persia.

One day Mordecai was sitting at his post by the palace gate and overheard two guards plotting to kill the king. Mordecai told Esther, and she told the king, who ordered the guards to be hanged and Mordecai's good deed to be recorded—but it was soon dropped out of mind. Later, the king's chief of staff, Haman, manipulated the king into sealing an edict requiring everyone to bow to him. When Mordecai refused, Haman became enraged and extracted from the king a second order to annihilate all of the Jews. Haman, a descendant of Amalek, probably wasn't aware that he was continuing an ancient enmity between his ancestors and the Jews. And the king was unaware that it was a gross, anti-Semitic lie that led him to give such a decree against the Jews.

When Mordecai discovered the plot, he was so grieved that he and the Jewish people tore their clothes, put on sackcloth and ashes, and went out into the city. However, Mordecai only went as far as the king's gate. When Esther heard about it, she sent Mordecai some clothes to change into, but he refused. Then she sent a messenger requesting that Mordecai put an end to the mourning. However, Mordecai sent back the details of Haman's plot and a note requesting that Esther go in to see the king about it. Esther was called to make a choice.

Mordecai's request was a costly request, but Esther could not avoid making a choice one way or the other. She sent back a message by her servant, Hatach, that she couldn't go to see the king. She reminded Mordecai that going in to see the king unscheduled could result in her death. The only exception to this was if the king extended his golden scepter to spare her life. It was a very serious risk that Mordecai was asking her to take. I am reminded of what Jesus said: "If any man will come after me, let him deny himself, and take up his cross daily, and follow me" (Luke 9:23, NIV).

When Mordecai received Esther's message, he replied, "Do not think in your heart that you will escape in the king's palace any more than all the other Jews. For if you remain completely silent at this time, relief and deliverance will arise for the Jews from another place, but you and your father's house will perish. Yet who knows whether you have come to the kingdom for such a time as this?" (Esther 4:13-14, NKJV).

Esther wanted to resolve the problem without getting involved in the conflict. But conflict is a burden of the anointed. She did not need to fear conflict, for she had been anointed to handle it.

How many times have you and I avoided confronting people because we want to avoid conflict, only to have things get worse? We fail to realize that God has not given us a task that he has not equipped us to handle. I am reminded of Paul's word to Timothy: "For God hath not given us the spirit of fear; but of power, and of love, and of a sound mind" (2 Timothy 1:7).

Esther's anointing, as followed by hard and risky choices, is not unique to her. Let's look at Joseph, the dreamer. He was favored by his father, Jacob, and anointed by God. But he was hated by his brothers. They resented Joseph so much that they threw him in a pit and sold him into bondage. Yet everywhere Joseph went, God's anointing and favor followed. He rose and found favor in Potiphar's house. He could have accepted Mrs. Potiphar's intimate offer, but his anointing demanded the costly choice of a conviction and a prison term. And even in prison Joseph found favor and was given charge over the other inmates. Joseph's ability to interpret dreams caused him to find favor with Pharaoh, and he became a chief administrator. God positioned Joseph so that during famine he was able to help the very brothers who had tried to kill him. In the faith of an anointed one, Joseph declared, "But as for you, ye thought evil against me; but God meant it unto good" (Genesis 50:20). Joseph was able to face conflict because he knew that God's anointing was still with him.

Still another anointed biblical "case history" concerns a young shepherd boy named David. Judge Samuel shocked David when he was called from among his sheep and anointed (see 1 Samuel 16:12). He was quite young, but it was awesome, and he never forgot it. David was never the same after that. He felt led to fight the Philistine giant, Goliath, because the name of Jehovah was insulted. *Some*body had to stand up for the Lord. David dared to take the risk. King Saul wanted David to reduce the risk by wearing armor in battle, but David, small as he was, chose to follow God's call by using only what God had given him. He had only a slingshot and five smooth stones. But using what the Lord gave him, David was able to kill Goliath. To the surprise of friend and foe, David had been equipped to face his conflict. In fact, God *always* equips the anointed, no matter how risky or seemingly impossible the assigned task.

Look now at one final model and case history: There was a prophetess and judge in the Old Testament named Deborah. She was the fourth and only female judge of Israel, and she was surely anointed by God. God told her to send for Barak and instruct him to gather 10,000 men from Naphtali and Zebulun and lead the way to Mount Tabor. God promised to lure Sisera, the commander of Jabin's army, with his chariots and his troops, to the Kishon River and give Sisera into Barak's hands. But Barak was not confident and refused to go unless Deborah went with him. Deborah warned him, "I will surely go with thee: notwithstanding the journey that thou takest shall not be for thine honour; for the LORD shall sell Sisera into the hand of a woman" (Judges 4:9). As the anointed Deborah had prophesied, Sisera was killed, and God gave the Israelites the victory through a woman. As improbable and unpredictable as this victory seemed, God was once again overcoming huge odds and supporting those who obeyed the call that comes with anointing.

Tribulation, affliction, anguish, burdens, persecution, and trouble all go with the territory called anointing. There is no trophy without a contest; no victory without a battle; no rainbow without some showers; and no crown without a cross. All of these people had undaunted faith in God and courage against great odds that were rewarded with victories they had not the imagination to think up.

As we return to Esther, to conclude our survey of some of God's anointed, we see her firmly determined to risk the trip to the king. With a touch of triumphant sternness in her determination, she declared, "If I perish, I perish, but I'm going to see the king" (Esther 4:16, author's paraphrase). The risk inherent in her calling had only briefly been considered. Going to the palace was a done deal, regardless of what it might cost.

When she got there, it was no great surprise that God had already prepared the way for her. The king stretched forth the golden scepter and welcomed her to his royal court. Her request was granted, and the people she had been anointed and called to save were indeed saved. Hallelujah!

Modern Mordecais relay the call to every one of us: "Who knows whether *you* are called for just such a time and place as this?" The needs are great, and they confront us everywhere, but the same gracious God who appoints also anoints and empowers. When we accept and affirm our anointing, we can claim the promises made later to Isaiah—"Fear not: for I have redeemed thee, I have called thee by thy name" (Isaiah 43:1)—and repeated in one of the great hymns of the Church, "How Firm a Foundation":

> When through the deep waters I call thee to go,
> The rivers of sorrow shall not overflow;
> For I will be with thee thy trials to bless,
> And sanctify to thee thy deepest distress.

When the Manna Ceases

BY HENRIETTA CARTER

*And the manna ceased on the morrow after they had eaten
of the old corn of the land; neither had the children of
Israel manna any more; but they did eat of the fruit of the
land of Canaan that year.*
(Joshua 5:12)

Manna was the bread provided directly by God's divine power for the children of Israel after their exodus from Egypt. In our text, it appears at first glance that God has ceased to provide food for his people: "And the manna ceased on the morrow after they had eaten of the old corn of the land" (Joshua 5:12). But then the text goes on to say, "No manna appeared that day, and it was never seen again. So from that time on the Israelites ate from the crops of Canaan" (5:12, NLT). From all accounts, the manna had been significantly replaced with corn.

Before all of this, the Israelites had been brought safely out of Egypt and had journeyed for over a month in the wilderness. They began to murmur against Moses and against Aaron: "Would to God we had died . . . in the land of Egypt, when we sat by the flesh pots, and when we did eat bread to the full; for ye have brought us forth into this wilderness, to kill this whole assembly with hunger" (Exodus 16:3). So the LORD spoke to Moses, "Behold I will rain bread from heaven for you; and the people shall go out and gather a certain rate every day" (16:4).

The next morning, when the dew disappeared, thin white flakes, like frost, covered the ground. Puzzled, the children of Israel asked, "What is it?" Moses answered, "This is the bread which the LORD hath given you to eat" (Exodus 16:15). From that point on, the manna rained down from heaven six days a week, fifty-two weeks a year, for forty years. The Israelites had just one responsibility: to be obedient to God's instructions. Each man was to go outside his tent with an omer—a two-quart container—and gather enough for each person in his household. They were blessed with the bread of heaven. Yet they soon tired of it, lost their appetites, and began to complain. In the end, they loathed the manna altogether.

Once in the Promised Land, the manna ceased, and the Israelites were to eat of the fruit of the land of Canaan. Their new staple, corn, involved greater and more continuous labor than taking a container and gathering what had fallen from heaven. This was not an issue for the first year, because they could eat the corn that had been left behind by the Canaanites, but eventually they would have to work for their food. While the corn was still the provision of God, the children of Israel would now have to take personal responsibility for growing it. God upped the ante; it was time for them to grow up. The new land called for a new way of surviving. God had substituted the miracle of the manna with something different but equally as marvelous.

There are several important lessons to be learned from this text. First, there will be times when we have to live our lives under drastically changed conditions. Sometimes the change is for the better. It may be a job with great potential for advancement, generous pay, and excellent benefits. It may be an inheritance that brightens our financial situations. Perhaps we will meet and marry our helpmate, leading to a new home, security, and happiness.

There are also times when things change for the worse. We may experience seasons when the manna appears to have ceased, when the things we are accustomed to receiving with little or no effort are no longer available. It may be losing the health plan that was a part of our employment package and how we're faced with paying for our own medical insurance—or going without and praying that no one in our families becomes ill or in immediate need. It may be losing certain liberties that we once took for granted, like walking into a government building without showing identification, going through metal detectors, or having our bags searched in the name of national, state, or local security.

Perhaps it's the disappearance of rent-stabilized apartments that once provided low- and middle-income families with affordable housing. As the rents climb, so do the number of homeless in shelters and on the streets. It may be a tragedy, such as when, in a matter of minutes on one clear, crisp September morning, twin towers fell, taking with them thousands of lives, jobs, homes, and an entire nation's sense of peace, confidence, and security.

No matter what the change may be or how happy it may make us, we are required to grow up, to be mature enough to handle our newfound privileges. No matter what the change may be, no matter how the manna ceases, we will come to realize that God's provisions are being directed in new and different ways.

What *really* happens when our manna ceases—or is manifested in a way that requires us to engage in intense struggle, effort, prayer, and labor? Do our joys cease as well? Think about it! In our childhood and youth we depended on our parents to provide for our every physical and emotional need. We looked to our teachers to help us grow in knowledge and wisdom, in the three R's. Eventually we grew up, bid farewell to our teachers, moved out of our parents' homes, and began the challenging journey toward self-reliance, independence, and the exercise of sound judgment. We had to take personal responsibility for our survival—and the mistakes we would make along the way. The manna had ceased, so to speak. We were suddenly living in changed conditions, whether good or bad. Yet God was there to feed us in new ways. We can trust that God will supply our needs when the manna ceases.

When the manna ceases, there is a second lesson for us to learn: Matters might get worse instead of better. This change could test our faith and require courage to work through the struggles that we encounter. The change might be the death of the head of the household. It may be a fire that leaves us homeless. It may be an illness that lands us in the hospital with mounting medical bills. It may even be a "pink slip" that leaves us without a regular source of income. Whatever the struggle, it is often painful and distressing. Where we once enjoyed God's provisions with very little effort on our part, where our testimony used to be "I'm blessed and highly favored," it now appears that these provisions have vanished and our resources have dried up. How can we bring ourselves out of these losses?

Notice I said that it *appears* that the supernatural has vanished. Believe me, God has simply substituted one miracle for another. My brothers and my sisters, no matter in what manner God works, God does work! Manna or corn, it's all God's work. God demonstrated his provision for the children of Israel through supernatural means. He became a pillar of cloud by day and a pillar of fire by night. When they tried to escape from Pharaoh, God came to their defense, opening up the Red Sea. When they were thirsty and had no water, he gave them water from a rock and made bitter water sweet. He sent quail when they hungered for meat and rained manna from heaven when they needed bread. But after all the blessings, they were told that they would have to provide for themselves by the toil of their hands. They would have to use their God-given gifts, talents, and abilities.

And so it is with us. The beginning of our Christian walk often requires the constant supernatural support of our heavenly Father. But as we grow and develop, we are expected to invest our God-given time, talent, and treasure in doing what we can for ourselves. Beloved, my brothers and my sisters, our awesome God does not waste his resources. He will not do for us what he has gifted and empowered us to do for ourselves.

And that brings me to the final lesson we can learn from the manna: Whether matters get better or worse, the end of the story brings a promising new beginning with God. Instead of looking to God to provide for us without any effort on our part, we can now take responsibility for our lives and whatever we accomplish to make for a more joyful and fulfilling life in God's kingdom.

How bountiful are our blessings! When Jesus came to live on earth, he wrought miracles in abundance. His life on earth brought peace and joy to all whose lives he touched. His love was shared abundantly. After his death and resurrection, the Church became firmly established and the truth of the gospel was made evident by its renewing power. The miracles were not nearly as frequent. Believers learned to walk by faith and not by sight. The acts of healing and deliverance were experienced in new ways. And the gospel has spread wherever God's children live. We hear the joyful sound: Jesus lives!

Our own church, in her early years, was largely supported by our denomination. But she grew up. God prospered her and empowered her to invest tithes, talents, and treasures in becoming a self-supporting, "Great Commission" church. God began feeding us in new ways. He sent anointed leaders to preach the gospel and to bring men and women into a saving knowledge of Christ. We discovered our gifts and began to use them. The prayers of faith became tools for deliverance and freedom from bondage. The church grew into a Holy-Spirit-empowered entity, fulfilling her mission to "glorify God, win souls, and nurture people through worship, teaching, preaching, in fellowship, and discipleship."

Although the manna ceased with the end of financial support from our denomination, we discovered that God simply substituted one miracle for another. God was—and remains—with us, as he promised. God, who loves us so much that he gave us his only begotten Son, is as almighty as ever. He still performs miracles. He still opens closed doors. While God provides manna in our wilderness and water during our seasons of desert travel, there comes a time when we need to do what our hands find to do. We will continue to make the best use of the resources God has given to us. God will do the rest. As it is sometimes said, "Man's extremities are God's opportunities."

When we could not save ourselves, God helped us. God sent us a Savior, Jesus, his only begotten son. Whether God provides by supernatural or by natural means, all of it is our most powerful Creator's will and way. When the manna ceases, we know that God may change his source of supply, but that no matter with what or when, God will always provide for his children's needs!

Leah: Rejected but Not Forgotten

BY NANCY CRAWFORD SANDERS

*And when the LORD saw that Leah was
hated, he opened her womb.*
(Genesis 29:31)

The Bible speaks of many women; some have names, others don't. Many of us, from time to time, have difficulty naming even a tenth of the Bible's women or their involvement in the salvation plan of God. Yes, I have always been fascinated with how the stories of the women in the Bible have so thoroughly been hidden. Most of the time, we can't feel their pain, their alienation, or their rejection.

Leah, in this twenty-ninth chapter of Genesis, is introduced to us by way of Jacob, the son of Isaac. You really can't talk about Leah without mentioning Jacob, because, like so many women even today, Leah's personhood seemed to have significance only as it was in some way connected with a man, Jacob.

So come with us, as the Spirit and I, in consecrated imagination, invite you to join us in a front-row seat and begin to share this story. It all began in a place called Canaan, where Jacob, along with his mother Rebekah, had plotted to steal his older brother Esau's birthright. In order for Jacob to escape the wrath of Esau, Rebekah sent Jacob to Haran, where her brother Laban lived. Once Jacob made it to Haran, the first person he met was Rachel, his uncle Laban's daughter, who at the time was watering her father's flock.

Rachel was the younger of Laban's two daughters. The older was Leah. The recorder of this narrative was very descriptive of the women. Leah had weak eyes. One could surmise that she was cross-eyed or had very bad eyesight, or maybe it could mean that her eyes were not attractive, that they lacked sparkle. Rachel, on the other hand, was radiantly beautiful and well-formed.

From the moment Jacob saw Rachel, he fell in love with her. It was his desire to marry her. Since Jacob ran away from home with no means of supporting himself, he made his uncle a proposition: Jacob would offer Laban seven years of free labor in exchange for Rachel's hand in marriage. Laban readily agreed to this customary proposition.

When the seven years had passed, Jacob told his uncle, "Give me my wife, for my days are fulfilled" (Genesis 29:21). The Bible is silent on Laban's response to Jacob's request, and the silence certainly suggests a sinister plan to deceive Jacob instead of a vocal commitment to follow through on his promise. Time was of the essence for Laban. He hurriedly invited family, friends, and neighbors to a wedding feast. And on the night of the wedding, he substituted Leah for Rachel. Leah was heavily veiled, and the tent to the wedding chamber was completely darkened. There was very little conversation, as was customary during this time, and Jacob had no clue as to the deception he was about to uncover. It wasn't until morning that Jacob made the cruel discovery: Behold, his wife was Leah.

Leah's story is not recorded to give the reader pleasure in human suffering, but to offer realistic insight into the human condition and the ways in which God intervenes. The realism of the story reaches its peak when, after the deception on the wedding night, the fact that Jacob began to despise Leah is not edited out. He no doubt hated the deception he saw in Leah, for she too had cooperated fully in Laban's conspiracy. He forgot that he had defrauded his own brother, so he had the nerve to despise Leah.

"But when the LORD saw that Leah was hated, he opened her womb" (29:31). God was aware of her unjust treatment and deep pain. God's justice wanted Leah to be blessed with progeny, to brighten her world of brokenness. So also, God sees us in our alienation. In our distress of mind and emotions, God sees us. In our isolation and our fear, God sees us. "For I know the thoughts that I think toward you, saith the LORD, thoughts of peace, and not of evil, to give you an expected end" (Jeremiah 29:11).

There is nothing that anyone can do to avoid rejection, but whenever we do experience it, we must avoid internalizing it and opening the door to low self-esteem. We don't have to become people-pleasers, always trying to fit in and gain the approval of others. Leah had no control over the way Jacob felt about her. The Bible never once tells us that it was anything specific and capable of change, like her looks, that caused him to reject her. One could surmise that, from her childhood, Leah had always been overlooked, causing her to be vulnerable to rejection and a deep sense of unworthiness. Her deficit in self-worth was unfortunately hinged on how other people saw her.

The human need for love was never satisfied for Leah by the three people who were most important in her life: Jacob, Laban, and Rachel. Only God saw Leah's need for self-worth; God saw her pain and her brokenness and said to Leah, "I love you just the way you are."

Isn't it just like God to move into the arena of our struggles and confront the distress, loneliness, and lostness of our lives in order to bring us hope? It has been said that hope is the living awareness of God's providence. If God had not stepped in, Leah would have remained in her hopeless state. But God overruled her plight. God offered relief and hope, allowing Leah's thinking to move forward. God transformed her predicament as well as her state of mind. Leah had been fighting so desperately to fit in, when God had called her to stand out.

Two things God wanted for Leah, and they were liberation and celebration. Only God could liberate her, set her free in her mind and her spirit. No cosmetic surgery for Leah, only a transformation by the renewing of her mind. Now, celebration must come from Leah. Both liberation and celebration must be held in interactive tension. Each needs the other. Each becomes unbalanced without the other. Leah's celebration did not rise by its own power. Her celebration responded to the intervention of God. Leah may have been despised by her husband, envied by her sister, and exploited by her father, but she was loved by her God.

Leah's life story gives us the impression that she never experienced the sweetness of married life. Every day she just lived her secondary role, only to see her own husband comfort Rachel by smiling, favoring, loving, and respecting her. However, as our text records, "When the LORD saw that Leah was hated, he opened her womb." God overruled the negativity that held Leah for so many years. She had two strikes against her: One, she was unattractive; and two, she was unloved by her husband. Nevertheless, she was fertile and her sister was not. Poor Rachel was barren, but Leah had sons.

Leah had been in a bad set of circumstances, and God didn't completely change this. God changed *Leah* by giving her grace to live in a less-than-perfect situation. God compensated for the strikes against her by empowering her to give birth. And even this was further supplemented by the fact that the offspring were *boys*, multiplying her joy in childbirth. God gave Leah some boys. She gave birth to four sons in rapid succession, having a final total of six. In her world, in her day, there was no better blessing to be had.

Leah gave birth to boys whom God would use mightily in the salvation plan. All six of her sons became progenitors of six whole tribes: Reuben, Simeon, Levi, Judah, Issachar, and Zebulun. Two of these stood out further from the rest in the annals of history. One son was Levi, progenitor of the tribe of Levi. Out of his family line came the three orders of the Levitical priesthood. They would become the teachers of the law for the nation of Israel for the rest of time. Moses and Aaron were members of these orders. Another outstanding son was Judah, ancestor of David, and thus of Jesus.

We seldom, if ever, talk of Leah in these terms, but in many significant places in the history of Judaism we could say in all truth, "I'm talking about Leah's boys." Of all the mothers in the Old Testament, none had so many sons to be proud of. None were so pivotally and prominently placed in the genealogy of the Old Testament.

Jesus came that the Leahs of the world might have joy in the midst of their sorrow. Leah's descendant, Jesus, came that what so often looks like cosmic injustice might be compensated for by the gracious providence of God.

Leah's body was strengthened to bring forth children, and her spirit was made glad by the knowledge that God cared. After the birth of Judah, Leah cried forth, "Now will I praise the LORD!" (Genesis 29:35). After the birth of every one of her sons, starting with Reuben, she might well have burst out with the song of praise later made famous by Jesus' mother, Mary: "My soul doth magnify the Lord, and my spirit hath rejoiced in God my Saviour. For he hath regarded the low estate of his handmaiden: for, behold, from henceforth all generations shall call me blessed" (Luke 1:46-48).

Our text cries out to the "Leah Left-Outs" of the world, "God sees *your* plight, too, and God cares. God's justice and mercy are on their way to your aid. They'll be there in due season." Praise the Lord! Hallelujah!

Come Out and Stay Out!

BY ELAINE McCOLLINS FLAKE

But Paul, being grieved, turned and said to
the spirit, I command thee in the name of Jesus Christ to
come out of her. And he came out the same hour.
(Acts 16:18)

O ne of the travesties of the human condition is the reality that there are segments of humanity committed to the oppression and margin- alization of other humans. There are those who will wholehearted- ly work to ensure that other humans live in states of mental, physical, and emotional bondage, because when others are in bondage and living on the "outside," they benefit. In this world, the economic strength of many cultures or many people within the culture is dependent on another group or groups of people living on the backside of life.

While a member of Congress, my husband often told me how many of the small, economically strapped areas in upstate New York would lobby for the building of prisons in their area. The building of prisons would bring much-needed jobs and contracts to the area and would provide the fiscal shot in the arm that their communities needed. Of course, the tragedy of this request is that in asking for a prison, they want prisoners. They are essentially looking for the just and unjust incarceration of the poor, uneducated, and socially neglected to popu- late the institution. The need for money blinds them to a consciousness that would seek to institute less profitable schools or programs designed to build human dignity and quality of life. They are willing and eager to go to the bank on the misery of black, Latino, and white men and women.

To be sure, many a child of God has fallen prey to individuals and systems that willingly contribute to our hurt, bondages, and unfulfilled living. We have contended with friends, significant others, family members, employers, and politicians who were truly vested in keeping us emotionally bound, economically strapped, physically confined, and professionally restricted. Women, in particular, have struggled against patriarchy in the academy, workplace, and church, and then had their personal relationships complicated by men who wanted nothing more than to control their minds and money for personal gain. Financiers have robbed black land owners in the South by forcing them out of homesteads they later developed and made millions on. And, moreover, doctors perform unnecessary hysterectomies, clinics peddle abortions, and politicians take money from underprivileged communities and put it in more privileged communities where the campaign contributions are larger. Sadly, capitalism, racism, and sexism have produced those whose commitment to personal gain transcends human compassion and sensitivity.

Women of color know volumes about oppression; we have lived with it, we have been hurt by it, and we have prayed to be free of it. We have come out of it, only to return by a different way. But the Lord would have us embrace the reality that as we answer God's call to divine purpose and human fulfillment, we have a moral and spiritual obligation to reject and separate from the oppressive forces in our lives. We must vigilantly seek God-given insight, wisdom, and truth that empowers us to identify every situation, individual, or attitude that has the potential to oppress and suppress that person in us who was born to soar.

Oppression can be defined as anything or anyone that hinders or compromises the abundant and productive life to which God has called all of us. It is that subtle or overt physical, mental, or emotional restriction that denies personal fulfillment and growth. It is that area of bondage that robs a woman or man of authentic living and robs God of the glory that belongs to God.

One of the most devastating things that can happen to a person or a people is for the oppressors to become so shrewd and cunning that the reality of their oppression escapes them or they *lose their commitment to personal freedom and human dignity.* When women accept disrespect from their men and children, and when they do not challenge those who deprive them of human dignity, they consent to and participate in their own oppression. When females are casual about their men calling them "bitches," and when city dwellers contribute to their own substandard living by littering their own communities and defacing their own surroundings, we see a self-imposed oppression that contributes to the profit of record companies and slumlords.

But, Acts 16:16-23 reminds us that the hour has come for the people of God to intensify their pursuit for personal and corporate freedom. The Bible says that Paul, Silas, and the other missionaries were on their way to the place of prayer when they were met by a slave girl who was controlled by an ungodly spirit and ungodly men. We know very little about this young girl, but one thing of which we are sure is this: *She was not her own woman.* We are told that her owners made a great deal of money by prostituting the girl's fortune-telling gift.

It would appear from the reading of this text that the slave girl was sadly resolved to her oppression. Like many oppressed women, she probably did not know how to really move away from the forces that had her bound. But it is apparent that God moved her to behavior that resulted in her liberation. The writer tells us that for *some reason* she was compelled to call attention to herself as the men of God moved through the city on that day and the days that followed.

He says that as they went from place to place, the girl followed them, shouting, "These men are servants of the Most High God, who are telling you the way to be saved" (16:17, NIV). It is amazing that in her oppressed state she recognized truth and power. This distressed female was captivated by the Holy Spirit that was setting people free around her. The Spirit of the Holy God, who is committed to the liberation of all flesh, was apparently drawing her to a new life in Jesus. We would have to believe that her taunts were a cry for help, a cry for a better way of living.

For days she cried out, and when she finally commanded Paul's attention, he turned to her and cried out, "In the name of Jesus Christ I command you to come out of her!" (16:18, NIV). And the Bible says that at that moment, *the ungodly spirit left her, and she was set free.*

This should have been a day of jubilation, but there were some who did not rejoice. For her owners, the spiritual and mental release of this ungodly spirit meant a loss of income, and they could not celebrate her liberation. Rather, they were outraged and had the apostles jailed. But the good news is that in spite of all that the men did, the bondage of the woman was over. They resisted, they made a ruckus, but it did not matter. In spite of human protests, she was free and the power of God overruled their callous disregard for human dignity. She had come out, and my faith tells me that her relationship with the Savior empowered her to progressively walk in that freedom. *She who the Son set free was free indeed.*

The message of this text is that God hears the cries of the oppressed and is committed to empowering them to walk away from their captivity. God is calling for the church to stop submitting to oppressive forces and, moreover, to make the necessary investment to participate in the liberation of others. It is time to choose some different roads. It is time to let God close some of the doors that will lead to destruction and open the doors that will lead you to the purposes of God. There are some states of being that contribute to the aborting of our divine callings, and, for our sakes and the sake of the kingdom, we must identify and eliminate them.

The yokes of childhood trauma, family victimization, spiritual abuse, and sexual violence are strong, but we can be set free through the power of God. We are empowered to stand in the midst of those forces that seek to steal who we are in God. We should be all that God wants us to be, and all that others need us to be.

You who are oppressed are privileged to call out to God for your salvation. You who need a better life and want power to move through the difficulties you face, pray to our Lord God in season and out of season. Hold on to God persistently until you arrive at your liberation. Keep the faith and believe that our Lord will bring you out and will also provide the way for you to stay out. To God be the glory! Amen.

That's Love!

BY FLEETA TURRENTINE

*When Jesus therefore saw his mother, and the
disciple standing by, whom he loved, he saith unto
his mother, "Woman, behold thy son!" Then saith
he to the disciple, "Behold thy mother!"*
(John 19:26-27)

The awesome day of Jesus' crucifixion had arrived. Some of the disciples had gathered with the mourning crowd of women. Mother Mary and the other Marys had been with Jesus on that triumphant "Hosanna" march only days before. They had been with him through the arrest and the trial, and now they were there to witness that cruel and unusual experience of death on a cross.

In his litany of brief utterances that Jesus spoke from the cross, the one word he expressed that was not directed to us, but specifically to the woman who brought him into the world and to his dearest friend on earth, is an exposition of his selflessness. This precious personal expression that was uttered by Jesus in the quaking hour of his death bequeaths a deep love and concern for his mother and his friend, which extends far beyond his concern for himself. This third word, which does not appear to have the universal appeal of some of the more prophetic utterances included in Jesus' seven last words, does, however, offer an answer for the human quandary. In the Old Testament, Cain asked the question, "Am I my brother's keeper?" (Genesis 4:9). On the cross at Calvary, Jesus answers the question: "Woman, behold thy son!" Then saith he to the disciple, "Behold thy mother!" (John 19:26-27). Yes, indeed we are our brother's keepers, our mother's keepers, and indeed we are responsible for the care, best interest, and well-being of one another, of all of God's children.

The aim of the enemy is to divide and conquer. Jesus bridges the gap for the entire human race as he confirms the reality of the extended family beyond gender, beyond generations, and beyond genetics, there on the cross at Calvary.

What are the dynamics of gender at the cross? Let us note that Jesus says to Mary, "*Woman*, behold your son." He does not say "Mom, Mother, Mama, behold your son." His use of the word *woman* is symbolic of an affection, a love that speaks to humankind in the ultimacy of the creation of Adam and Eve before they ate of the fruit. It lends itself to a love much deeper than that of a fleshly nature and recreates the core of the love that God had intended for the world. This love moves beyond a lust for the flesh or a romantic encounter to a love for personhood and an eternal love for one another that only an intimacy with God can create, bless with understanding, and sustain.

This love does not end in divorce or in the waking morning hours of a one-night stand. This is not the kind of love referred to when a sistah might say, "Girl, that man melts my butter and pops my corn!" No, my brothers and my sistahs, this is not a love that embraces the ideology that women are from Venus, and men are from Mars! This is not a love that embraces classism and seeks to marginalize women to a lower socio-economic status—or to no status at all. Nor is it a love that promotes sexism, where men prey on women for sexual favors. This love moves beyond gender and embraces oneness!

Not only does Jesus word from the cross extend beyond gender; it extends beyond generations. Here was the mother of Jesus, an elderly woman in her golden years, having already traversed years of hardship and blessing, sorrow and joy, being contrasted against this disciple John, this youthful, timid boy, full of energy, expectation, and curiosity for life.

The presence of Mary in this scene reminds us of our responsibility as mature adults to mentor our youth, to provide wise council to children who are lost in a world more concerned with technological advancement than with theological acumen and spiritual insight. Just yesterday, a sixty-five-year-old mother was bludgeoned to death by her daughter. On the other extreme, children live in homes where their mothers and their fathers are sexual predators. The abuse of elders and children is on the rise in our society today. I tell you, something has gone awry! Surely this is not what Jesus had intended. Children are being left home alone, forced to take on adult responsibilities; childhoods are truncated. Children are having children, and grandmothers are having to take sole responsibility for raising their grandchildren.

But it is not just a one-way street. While it is necessary for the older generation to offer wise council and positive role models for the younger generation, this word also suggests that youth have a responsibility to the elderly. Jesus says to John, "Behold your mother." Jesus infers the responsibility that John must accept for Jesus' mother. Our population of elderly in the United States is growing; people are living far longer than they did thirty years ago. The healthcare system is overrun by geriatric patients in need of caregivers. Our elderly are being tucked away in nursing homes and long-term care facilities—and forgotten! We make one visit to the sick and shut-in and consider our good deed done. We are in such a hurry these days that we don't have the patience to wait for an elderly person to change lanes on the highway; instead, we step on the gas and speed around them. Or we almost run over the heels of a senior in the grocery store with our shopping carts because they are not moving down the aisle at the same speed we are. We grumble about the time and the patience it takes to care for our aging parents.

We need to go back to the cross! It is our responsibility to respect and remember our elders, to honor our mothers and our fathers, and to keep alive the principals and integrity of our ancestors, who cared for their elderly until death, and who cared for us in infancy and childhood. When asked if I would preach today, I almost said no, because I had promised my mother that I would arrive in Los Angeles today, to spend the Easter weekend with her. So, after I finish this sermon, I will run and jump on a plane and fly down to Los Angeles to be with my mother, as I am her only child. She needs me, and I need her! Church, just like Jesus, we have a responsibility to love that extends beyond generational lines.

Finally, if this love, this affection, this word that Jesus gives at the cross extends beyond gender and extends beyond generations, then surely it extends beyond genetics. Mary and John were not family as we know family today. They were not biologically related; they were not created out of the same gene pool, yet they loved one another, and they loved Jesus.

Consider the love of Naomi and Ruth, or of Joshua and Moses! This was a love that reached beyond gender, beyond generations, and beyond genetics! Family is more than genetic. People who show compassion, patience, loyalty, and commitment are people who *become* our family. Hopefully, we all have friends who have listened when we were discouraged, visited and taken care of us when we were ill, remembered us on special occasions, overlooked our shortcomings, and forgiven our selfishness. In this poignant moment, Jesus reaches beyond genetics and embraces humankind at large—the community. Beyond the differences that separate us, we share one common humanity, and thus we belong to each other.

No, Mary and John were not related by a genetic bloodline, but they were related by the blood of Jesus. As Christians we embrace all races, all classes, all people—we become one in Christ! Yes, the love that Jesus showed at Calvary represents the unfailing love of God. It enables us to love our friends and our enemies. It inclines us to love those who falsely rise up against us.

We sing of the blood that Jesus shed for us way back on Calvary, and it was shed out of love. It soothes all our doubts and all our fears, and it washes away all our tears; it was shed because of love. It reaches to the highest mountain, it flows to the lowest valley, and it gives us strength from day to day, just because of that unfailing love which will never lose its power. The love that gave the blood that Jesus shed for you and for me way back on Calvary extends beyond gender, extends beyond generations, and extends beyond genetics.

What kind of love was this, this love Jesus gave to his mother and his disciple John? This love ran so deep in his veins that in the midst of his torment and his suffering, in all of his pain and anguish, his thirst and his feelings of forsakenness, he sought to bestow this love upon his mother and his disciple John.

What manner of love does it take to transcend hate and cruelty, abuse and scorn, slander and shame? What kind of love would stand up under the brutality of nail-pierced hands and a crown of thorns? What kind? I can't imagine such a love except for Jesus! What kind of love? I know no other kind than Jesus' kind. That's love! I dare not try to give such love without Jesus. That's love! The blood that Jesus shed for me way back on Calvary. That's love! The blood that Jesus shed showed love for all of God's children. That's love!

About Those
Preaching Women

AUDREY BRONSON is an ordained minister who was consecrated as bishop in 1994. She established the Sanctuary Church of the Open Door in 1975 and is also founder of the Sanctuary Christian Academy, the Sanctuary Bible Institute, and the Sanctuary Counseling and Referral Center.

JO ANN BROWNING accepted the call to ministry in 1982 and has since 1983 served in pastoral team ministry with her husband at Ebenezer African Methodist Episcopal Church in Fort Washington, Maryland.

CECELIA WILLIAMS BRYANT has walked in a ministry to African and Diasporic women for over thirty years. As an ordained elder in the African Methodist Episcopal Church, she is the founder of the A.M.E. Church in the Ivory Coast and serves as Episcopal Supervisor of fifteen states in the Western U.S., where her husband, Rt. Rev. John R. Bryant, serves as Bishop.

HENRIETTA CARTER is the twenty-seventh pastor of the Mariners' Temple Baptist Church, New York City, where she shepherds both a Sunday congregation and a Wednesday Lunch Hour of Power congregation.

ELAINE MCCOLLINS FLAKE is an itinerant elder in the African Methodist Episcopal Church who currently serves as co-pastor, with husband Floyd H. Flake, of The Greater Allen Cathedral of New York. She is the author of the book God in Her Midst: Preaching Healing to Hurting Women.

LOIS B. FORTSON is an ordained elder in the West Ohio Conference of the United Methodist Church. She is a widow with four sons, three daughters-in-law, and seven grandchildren.

CHERYL TOWNSEND GILKES is assistant pastor (for special projects) of the Union Baptist Church, Cambridge, Massachusetts, and the John D. and Catherine T. MacArthur Professor of African-American Studies and Sociology at Colby College, Waterville, Maine. She is the author of the book If It Wasn't for the Women: Black Women's Experience and Womanist Culture in Church and Community.

BERNADETTE GLOVER-WILLIAMS, executive pastor of Cathedral International, loves ministry and delights in watching the faith come alive. She served as co-editor of the book Women at the Well II, published by Judson Press.

CAROLYN TYLER GUIDRY is a presiding elder and a candidate to become the second female bishop in the African Methodist Episcopal Church. She has been in ordained ministry for thirty-one years.

LISA ROXANNE HARRIS serves as associate executive minister of mission and stewardship for the Philadelphia Baptist Association, one of thirty-five regions of the American Baptist Churches USA.

JACQUELINE E. MCCULLOUGH is the founder and senior pastor of The Gathering at Beth Rapha in Pomona, New York. A songwriter, author, and recording artist, she conducts overseas medical missions in her native Jamaica, West Indies.

DIANE GIVENS MOFFETT is the associate pastor of the Elmwood United Presbyterian Church in East Orange, New Jersey. She is a preacher, teacher, and author of Beyond Greens & Cornbread: Reflections on African American Christian Identity, published by Judson Press.

LOIS A. POAG-RAY is pastor of the historic Pilgrim African Methodist Episcopal Church in Washington, D.C. A former professor of management at the University of the District of Columbia, she is also executive director of the Pilgrim A.M.E. Church Job Connection, Inc.

LISA D. RHODES is dean of Sisters Chapel and director of the Sisters Center for WISDOM (Women in Spiritual Discernment of Ministry) at Spelman College. She formerly served as assistant pastor at Ebenezer Baptist Church.

NANCY CRAWFORD SANDERS, an ordained American Baptist Minister, is associate minister of Calvary Baptist Church in Chicago, Illinois.

CASSANDRA A. SPARROW is an ordained itinerant elder on the ministerial staff of Lee Memorial African Methodist Episcopal (A.M.E.) Church in Kensington, Md., and Pilgrim A.M.E. Church in Washington, D.C. She is committed to the promotion of health and wholeness worldwide.

J. RUTH TRAVIS serves as a workshop leader at various retreats, conferences, and seminars in the areas of leadership and evangelism/discipleship training.

LILLIE LAWTON TRAVIS is pastor of the Walker Grove Missionary Baptist Church of Newington, Georgia, and is the first female pastor in the church's ninety-six-year history. She is also in demand as a preacher, lecturer, and conference leader on the topic of women in ministry.

FLEETA L. TURRENTINE is a chaplain at Alta Bates Summit Medical Center in Oakland, California. She is devoted to allowing God to use her as a vessel to pastor, teach, and preach to those are sick, walking in grief and loss, and in need of spiritual renewal.

CHERYL D. WARD is associate pastor at Memorial Tabernacle (Christ Holy Sanctified Church U.S.A.). She is the author of two nonfiction books and one novel.

RENITA J. WEEMS, PH.D., is the 2003–2005 William and Camille Cosby Visiting Professor of Humanities at Spelman College, Atlanta, Georgia. She is the author of several books, including the prestigious 1999 Wilbur Award-winning *Listening for God: A Minister's Journey through Silence* and *Doubt and What Matters Most: Ten Lessons in Living Passionately* from the Song of Solomon (Warner Brothers), released earlier this year.

LEAH E. WHITE is senior pastor of the Greater Faith Baptist Church in Baltimore, Maryland. She is much sought after as an anointed preacher, teacher, leadership developer, author, and motivational speaker.

ANGELA DEMPSEY WILLIAMS is the youth minister and minister in Christian education at Friendship Baptist Church in Atlanta.

BETTY WRIGHT-RIGGINS has served as a pastor, new church planter, Christian educator, and retreat and conference leader. Currently she serves as a member service representative for the Ministers and Missionaries Benefits Board of the American Baptist Churches, USA.

MARY H. YOUNG is an instructor in Christian education and interim director of the Doctor of Ministry Program at the Samuel DeWitt Proctor School of Theology, Virginia Union University, in Richmond, Virginia.